LANA TURNER

LANA TURNER

A Pyramid Illustrated History of the Movies

by
JEANINE BASINGER

General Editor: **TED SENNETT**

PUBLICATIONS
NEW YORK

LANA TURNER
A Pyramid Illustrated History of the Movies

A PYRAMID BOOK

Copyright © 1976 by Pyramid Communications, Inc.

Pyramid edition published December 1976

Library of Congress Catalog Card Number: 76-46168

Printed in the United States of America

Pyramid Books are published by Pyramid Publications (Harcourt Brace Jovanovich, Inc.) Its trademarks, consisting of the word "Pyramid" and the portrayal of a pyramid, are registered in the United States Patent Office.

PYRAMID PUBLICATIONS
(Harcourt Brace Jovanovich, Inc.)
757 Third Avenue, New York, N.Y. 10017

Layout and Design by ANTHONY BASILE

ACKNOWLEDGMENTS

No book on Lana Turner could get off to a good start without first mentioning Lou Valentino, the man who is unofficially known as "the world's number one Lana Turner fan." For all the help, information, good advice and encouragement given to me by Lou, I am truly grateful. I hope that he will feel this book is worthy of Miss Turner. I also hope it will be worthy of his own friendship to me.

Thanks for help with films to Steve Ross, Pat Moore, and Don Krim at United Artists, Gary Collins at Universal, Eric Spilker of Spilker Films, and to William K. Everson. And especially to Rhonda Bloom and Doug Lemza at Films, Incorporated who have both also given me ideas about Lana Turner.

Thanks generally to my editor, Ted Sennett, and to Mrs. Peter Arico, my typist. Thanks to all my students who brought me Turner articles, especially Jeffrey Lane who was intrepid in this regard. Thanks to Bob, Jeffrey, Michael, Howard and Roger—and everyone else who provided moral support, especially Will Holtzman and Doug McKinney.

The most thanks to my husband, John, who probably did more work on this book than I did . . . and to my daughter, Savannah, who this time wrote her own book and was too preoccupied to have to be patient.

Photographs: From the collection of Lou Valentino

CONTENTS

Lana Turner is an authentic American sex goddess—the real thing. In satins and diamonds and white fox furs, her image is one of undeniable glamour. Yet to capture her essence accurately, a statue of Lana Turner would have to be mounted on top of a drug store stool. Lana Turner was never one thing or the other. Not just glamorous, but also girlish. Not just a tigress, but also a kitten. At first, not only wholesome and good, but also a little bad. Later, not all bad, but more than a little good. She was as much the ice cream parlor as she was the perfumed boudoir. That's what made her so irresistible.

Although no one thinks of Turner as a child star, she started so young that she has to be counted among those the American public watched grow up on film. Like Judy Garland and Mickey Rooney, she was a student at Metro-Goldwyn-Mayer's little red schoolhouse where she spent all her time "fending off learning and fending off Mickey." Also like Garland and Rooney, she matured into a person whose private escapades kept her in the public eye nearly as often as her film roles. Unlike Garland, her private life survived those disasters, and unlike Rooney, she kept her professional career going, remaining a top star even today.

There is very little pre-movie history on Lana Turner. It is as if

INTRODUCTION: GOLDEN GIRL OF THE SILVER SCREEN

she were born on film stock. At the end of one of her films, *Portrait in Black*, this phenomenon is symbolized. In a striking finale to an otherwise bland film, Lana Turner is seen in an attic window with a look of anguish on her face. Suddenly frozen in that unfriendly frame, her visage is changed from a blonde, blue-eyed and expensively gowned woman into a colorless black-and-white image . . . and then down to a negative. Like the process of evolution in reverse, Lana Turner is reduced before our eyes back to her own origins through the camera process.

For many this scene appears to tell the whole truth about Lana Turner—that she is an image and nothing more. Adela Rogers St. Johns once said, "Let's not get mixed up about the real Lana Turner. The real Lana Turner is Lana Turner. She was always a movie star and loved it. Her personal life and her movie star life are one."

It is perhaps the ultimate tribute to Turner's glamour that anyone could believe that. Lana Turner was not always Lana Turner, but perhaps she always *thought* she was. A browse through the Turner scrap-books indicates she certainly always had a unique relationship with the camera. There is one familiar childhood photograph—the one that is always published, as if it were the only one ever taken. (It well might be the only one. Turner's childhood was every bit as unstable and deprived as Marilyn Monroe's. Unlike Monroe, Turner elected not to make it an issue.) In this picture, the little girl's hair has been frizzled to a fare-thee-well (presumably by the loving hands of her beauty shop mother). Her smile is radiant. She has drawn her coat around herself in a perfect copy of a mannequin's studied grace, spreading it open to reveal the dress underneath. One foot is set perfectly in front of the other, showing off the shabby shoes and the small rolled stockings. Hands clasped, jaunty as can be, the child has struck a pose. She has given the camera what it was looking for—a little touch of personality and a lot of cheesecake. Lana Turner at least always had an idea that she *might* be Lana Turner.

When Turner first started in films, she was more of a little girl than Shirley Temple ever was, less calculating, less aware of her power over men. She was like the prettiest girl in school, the one with the proud and fluid walk, the gleeful giggle, and the wrinkled-up nose. Some of her early film roles pre-sent her all dressed up with an up-swept hairdo, white fur and long gloves, yet looking like somebody's little sister out on a blind date, trying to pass herself off as a grownup. But although she was fresh and young, she was not exactly innocent. She was more the kid who went to the party where they ran out of cake and ice cream before they got to her. So she was on the lookout for her share, with an appetite that wasn't going to settle for a small portion of anything.

After her first years as a starlet passed, a transformation took place in Lana Turner's screen image that was also taking place in her private life. A lovely girl turned into a glamour queen, wise to the world, even cynical, but still retaining enough of that young lady the public had first met to make her delicious. She became the kind of woman that men most desired, dangerous in a thrilling way, but safe and companionable, too.

What was the secret of Lana Turner's success with men, both on and off screen? It wasn't just that she was gorgeous, blonde and blue-eyed, with a perfect figure. Others in Hollywood had those attributes too. Was it the way she walked, head up, chest out, hips swinging? Or was it her soft voice, like a child's? Or was it the way she looked at every man she met, as if he were the last man on earth? Or

that, even if he weren't, she'd choose him anyway? Movie-goers and real-life friends alike sensed in Turner a basic generosity and kindness, coupled with her sex appeal, that was best reflected in Clark Gable's description of her: "A man can like her as much as he could love her."

This popularity with men made Lana Turner a national treasure during World War II. A G.I. allegedly wrote to his mother that "somehow it is better to be fighting for Lana Turner than it is to be fighting for the Greater Reich." It was a sentiment even the Germans could well understand. President Roosevelt himself invited her to his annual birthday ball, and when she left early to go dancing elsewhere, he was heard to sigh, "I wish I were going along." Everybody in those years had the "Lana Turner Blues," a silly song written by two soldiers which said, "I get the morning papers bright and early/I gotta know where I can see that girlie/'Cause since that night at the corner movie, I've got those Lana Turner blues."

As a beginner, Lana Turner had a light touch. Properly developed, she might have become an elegant comedienne, not unlike Carole Lombard. (Gable understood that.) She had the humor, and she had the class. She could wear any type of clothes beautifully, and her hair looked good in any style or any color, blonde, platinum, red, brown, or black. She was relaxed and easy, with movements that were naturally sexy. She could back away from a man, look him over with a twinkle in her eye, and move right back in on him. She came to recognize a certain look in a man's eye. She put that knowledge to work in her screen characterizations. She could respond to it in an actor, or duplicate it for herself.

It was inevitable that a girl with Turner's looks wasn't going to stay poor and unknown. She had to end up jeweled and gowned. Turner might have become a little girl with no daddy but a sugar daddy; instead she earned her own living. Early in life she became accustomed to being the boss at home, as she was the person who paid the bills. She knew it was *her* looks and *her* talent that brought home the dollars. She began to take the role of aggressor in relationships, without feeling the slightest bit self-conscious. After all, she was Lana Turner. Why hang back and wait for the man to decide? She picked her own men ... and she could have her pick. Although totally feminine, Lana Turner was one of the first film stars to take the male prerogative openly for herself. In this regard, she was liberated. She was less a slave to sex than she was its master.

14

Comparing Turner to Elizabeth Taylor, it is clear that where Taylor was spoiled and dependent on men, Turner was spoiled and independent of them. She just happened to like them a lot. And she happened to make a lot of bad choices. For this—and for her liberated life style which did not recognize the double standard—Lana Turner was publicly denounced.

Magnetic and disturbing, a powerful image, Turner was not easily cast as she matured. The undercurrent of violence which seemed fatally linked to her sex appeal became more overt. Even when she was young, she was not believable as an ingénue. (Because there was no innocence in her . . . or because there was none in us?) She was not just another beauty. She was "Lana"—a name that despite her popularity never caught on as a name for babies. It belonged only to her.

Originally, Turner was groomed by Metro as a logical inheritor of Joan Crawford's roles. In the early stages of her career, Turner was cast as a common girl trying to make it across the tracks. But Turner, growing up in Hollywood, took the tinsel town too much into her pores to be believable in the hash house. After a certain point, she looked too rich, too polished, too elegant, too much the girl from Orchid City to bring off a rags-to-riches role. Whereas Crawford could suppress her glamour and reach into herself to find the memory of her humble origins, Turner appeared to cut loose her past. For the audience, it ceased to exist. She was their movie goddess—born and raised on film for their pleasure—the product of photogenesis.

Although she was a top professional with an uncanny camera instinct, Turner's opportunity to develop as an actress passed after a series of sensational events occurred in her private life. Because no one would take her seriously, no one would give her a serious part. Her screen roles began to reflect personal scandals, and, with three or four exceptions, the movies she played in were drivel. A good director could use her raw emotional power and guide her to a stunning performance, but she lost the opportunity to work with such directors. Her box-office power was used to carry weak films. She was a star too often hitched to a wagon.

Turner herself seemed almost to give up and settle for the world's definition of her. In this sense, she let herself be used. She accepted the roles which cast her as the ultimate in glamour and expensive sex. She became a *true* sex symbol—an actress who played small, symbolic roles in which the meaning of the character came from a source other than the script. The source was her own private life.

A great movie star develops a persona over a long career. It is an image that grows out of the roles he or she plays on film. Audiences begin to think the star *is* that person on the screen. They believe John Wayne is John Wayne or Cary Grant is Cary Grant. There is no Michael Marion Morrison or Archie Leach.

Lana Turner reversed the pattern. She began to act out her own life on the screen, making a myth and a ritual out of herself, not her image. She began to be cast only in roles that were symbolic of what the public knew—or thought they knew—about her as a person. She found herself speaking lines such as "I would be loved as a woman—not as a goddess" and "Do you think I should put in an elevator (to the bedroom)?" This ritualization isolated her from her own talent. The little girl who was a fizzy vanilla soda became a champagne cocktail . . . and then a frozen daiquiri.

Lana Turner came from nothing to become a film star at a very young age. Behind her was the escapist daydreaming of a lonely and poverty-stricken little girl. She became a star, the thing she most dreamed of, while she was still herself a dreamy girl. She survived

by detaching herself from reality—the life she took up in Hollywood was a fantasy life, both on screen and off. Instead of being a person who had to develop an image, Turner was an image who had to develop as a person, to grow up. For her this was a long and painful process that took place on the front pages of the world's newspapers. A process that the public hasn't yet caught on to.

People still say there is no real Lana Turner, only the movie star. Her story begins on the drug store stool, with the painful childhood swept away. As the years pass, the film roles and the real-life drama intermingle to the point of utter confusion. Was it Cheryl Crane that her busy life as a film queen isolated her from—or was it Sandra Dee? Was it in the small town of Peyton Place that she broke down on the witness stand—or was it in Hollywood? Lana Turner is the only film star that the public has said is truly too glamorous to be real. Others can be accepted as people, albeit exotic, beautiful people, but still, behind it all, people like us. Why not Turner?

Because, to the audience, she *is* a goddess. An authentic Hollywood goddess. Not just photogenic, but also photogenetic. She has grown up over the years, it seems, but we haven't.

18

Julia Jean Mildred Frances Turner—from the very beginning she was a little girl with a big name. Her origins were so humble that only an American Charles Dickens or a high-paid soap opera writer could do them justice. She received her basic education at the movies until the day she was old enough and voluptuous enough to switch from being *at* them to being *in* them. After that, her formal education was of the most casual sort, but her instruction in the ways of the world was post-graduate.

Judy Turner—apparently she was never known as Julia or Jean or Mildred or Frances, but only as "Judy" until she became "Lana" —was the first and only child of Virgil and Mildred Turner —a smooth-talking gambler and his teen-age wife. She was born in the little mining town of Wallace, Idaho, on February 8, 1920. ("Can a little girl from a small mining town in the West find happiness as . . . ?")

Virgil Turner is a character whose image is both vague and legendary. He is described as a handsome, soft-spoken man who originally came from Alabama, but who, after serving in World War I, drifted west, plying his various trades of miner, gambler, and bootlegger. According to his daughter, he was a lovely man who might have been an actor if he had the

A STAR THEY WON'T FORGET IS BORN

proper training, possessing a good singing voice, a gift of mimicry, and a natural ability for dancing. Her portrait of Virgil Turner offers a picture of the charming rogue, a scoundrel with a heart of gold. A sort of Rhett Butler. Or, more appropriately, a sort of Clark Gable.

There is no opportunity to verify Mr. Turner's charm, or even the basic facts of his life. Following an all-night crap game in San Francisco, sometime around Christmas, 1930, Virgil Turner was murdered. His bludgeoned body was found abandoned in a tough San Francisco neighborhood, with his left shoe and sock (where he was known to stash his winnings) missing. The crime was never solved.

Mildred Turner was the daughter of a Wallace, Idaho engineer, barely fourteen years old when she first met Virgil at a Wallace dance. Because of her age, her family disapproved of the relationship, but the couple eloped shortly after she was fifteen. The newlyweds lived an itinerant life which halted temporarily when they returned to Wallace for the birth of their only child in the cold winter of 1920.

The three Turners then drifted from place to place, job to job. In-

At the age of eight, in San Francisco

evitably, the couple separated and Mildred went to work in a beauty parlor, boarding Judy out with a family in Modesto, California. It was during this two-year period of her life that ten-year-old Judy Turner was told of her father's death, a shock which she has called the dominant influence in her life. She continued to board with the Modesto family until her mother accidentally learned she was being mistreated. The girl had not only been forced to do all the work of the house, but had also been beaten and deprived of what little her mother had been able to send. ("I was a scullery maid, a cheap Cinderella with no hope of a pumpkin," says Turner.)

Those were desperate years for Mildred Turner and her daughter. Times were bad generally, and for a woman with a child to support—and little education to fall back on—it was a rough life. Like everyone else in Depression America, they found escape together at the movies. Judy Turner is said to have lived a rich fantasy life. Certainly she didn't live a rich life of any other kind.

Finally, mother and daughter decided to take a chance on changing their fate by changing their address—to Hollywood, U.S.A. Mildred Turner took a job at the Lois Williams Beauty Salon, and little Judy was enrolled at Hollywood High School. Judy had moved so often that her education, at best, had been spotty. School bored her, so that whenever she could, she cut out and ran across the street to Currie's Candy and Cigar Store and had herself a quick coke.

There must be no one left in the world who hasn't heard the one about the little girl who was discovered sipping a strawberry soda in the drug store. About how the great big man walked up to her and said, "Little girl, how would you like to be in pictures? I can fix it." And about how she would like it, and he could and he did, and a star was born.

By now this story about Lana Turner's discovery is part of Hollywood's history. The true story is even more unbelievable—it's the one about the little girl who wasn't really discovered sipping a strawberry soda. She couldn't have afforded it. It was a coke. And it wasn't a drug store and she wasn't sitting on a soda fountain stool. It was just a little candy store across the street from the high school where she liked to stand and thumb through the movie magazines she couldn't afford to buy.

Accuracy is irrelevant. What counts is that Judy Turner was a gorgeous young girl, and Billy Wilkerson (editor of the movie trade paper, *Hollywood Reporter*), spotted her sometime in January 1936, and invited her to see him about a movie career. Fortified by her mother as a chaperone (she was only one month short of sixteen), Turner went to see Wilkerson, who sent her on to Zeppo Marx, a well-established Hollywood agent. The Marx agency signed her, and she began making the rounds of the studios. At first it looked as if it were going to be easy. Selznick gave her a bit part in one of his big budget films, a movie which (because this is a legendary story) just had to be called *A Star is Born*, the debut of Judy Turner in motion pictures.

A star *was* born, but it didn't happen overnight. Judy spent nearly a year making rounds and being rejected because she was inexperienced and couldn't act. ("I didn't say she could act," her agent bellowed at one casting director. "I said she could be a movie star.") She even made a test for the coveted role of Scarlett in *Gone With The Wind*, a test which reveals a big-eyed near-child with very little poise or ability, but whose voice is distinctively soft and whose face is strikingly pretty.

Finally, Judy Turner was taken to meet Mervyn LeRoy, the successful director of such films as *I Am A Fugitive From A Chain Gang*, *Little Caesar*, *Five Star Final*, and *Gold Diggers of 1933*.

LeRoy was looking for a fresh young girl—someone new—to play a small but key role in a film he was preparing. Based on the novel "Death in the Deep South" by Ward Greene, the film would star Claude Rains and would be re-titled *Murder In The Deep South*—the one-word change seeming to have more "oomph" at the box office. As soon as Mervyn LeRoy saw young Judy Turner walk through the door, he knew she was his girl. The role of Mary Clay required someone who was remarkably pretty and fresh as a daisy, but it also required sex appeal. That was something Judy Turner had in abundance. She got the part. ("I'll have to ask my mother," she solemnly warned LeRoy.)

LeRoy knew that the person cast as the young girl who is raped and murdered *must* leave a definite imprint in the audience's minds. The sight of the pretty young girl swinging happily down the street must, in only a few moments of running time, be powerful enough to keep the audience feeling the tragedy of her loss. They must want to see her again, too, just like the people in the film who mourn her loss enough to lynch the man they think murdered her. Turner fulfills the demands of this imagery, not through any acting skill, but through her remarkable physical

Young Lana, at the start of her career

qualities.

LeRoy's finished film is rarely seen today, due to legal entanglements. Turner's famous part in it, however, is included in almost every compilation film of Hollywood goodies. Her part was small. She is first seen in a business college classroom, a dark-haired and dimpled darling who is seductively asking the flustered male teacher to help her with her school work. For a beginner, she is remarkably professional and utterly distinctive. She is completely calm and in control when she takes her seat at the ice cream shop and smartly orders the gaping soda clerk, "Make mine a chocolate malted and drop an egg in it as fresh as you."

Turner's big moment is her famous walk from the soda fountain, down the street, and back to the school building (where she is raped and murdered—off screen). Only a few short minutes on film—but she carved a lifetime image out of it. Lana Turner was a beautiful young girl with a free-swinging walk. She conveyed a naturalness, a delicious thrill in her own beauty, a joy in the simple act of walking down the street with all eyes on her . . . hips swaying, buttocks jiggling, and breasts bouncing. One of her best assets was this marvelous walk, which some have attributed to her training at Metro-Goldwyn-Mayer. A look at this film reveals it to be nature's gift. Shoulders back and head held high, Turner is a beautiful—and unforgettable—sight to see.

The film itself is a dark portrait of prejudice at work in the American South and corruption in the American legal system. Its story is one of the most brutal portraits of America ever seen on film, well-acted by a strong cast which included Claude Rains in the lead role of a lawyer on-the-make, plus Edward Norris, Gloria Dickson, Allyn Joslyn, and Elisha Cook, Jr., in a small role as the guy Mary Clay stands up. ("That's the closest Elisha Cook ever got to Lana Turner," observed one modern viewer.)

After LeRoy decided to use Judy Turner, there was the question of what to do about her name. Certainly Julia Jean Mildred Frances could never be put on a theatre marquee—except perhaps at Radio City Music Hall—and Judy had no pizzazz. After a long deliberation in LeRoy's office, Judy herself suggested the name of Lana, to be pronounced "Lah-nah." She says she has no idea where she got it.* Lah-nah Turner sounded great, and

---

* Like everything else about Turner's beginning in films, the stories vary about who first suggested her unusual name. Turner herself now takes the credit.

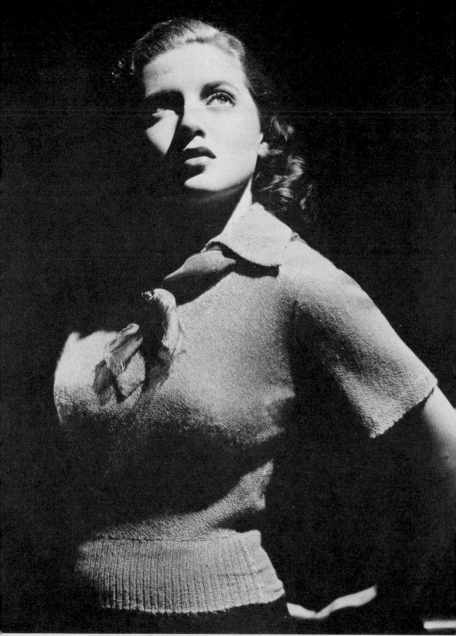

As Mary Clay in THEY WON'T FORGET (1937)

A starlet in the late thirties

THEY WON'T FORGET (1937). With Linda Perry

everyone agreed that would be it. And as if the show business gods were watching over the entire proceedings, another name change also took place. *Murder In The Deep South* became *They Won't Forget*—the perfect title for the film in which Lana Turner took a long walk toward stardom.

Several years ago, Lana Turner began denying the legend that she was discovered on a soda fountain stool, pointing out that the little shop across the street from Hollywood High was far less

glamorous than that. *They Won't Forget* proves her wrong. Her real discovery took place in *that* drugstore and on *that* stool. Sitting behind the counter, coyly confessing, "You know I can't stay mad," the lovely young Turner captured the attention of the true discoverers of stars—the American movie-going public.

A star nobody would forget *had* definitely been born. At a soda fountain, on a high stool, wearing a sweater and sipping a soda. The legend can stand.

In June, 1937, Lana Turner and her mother, thrilled out of their minds, attended the preview of *They Won't Forget* at the Warner Brothers Hollywood Theater. According to Turner, when they saw her famous walk and heard the audience reaction, they "scrooched" down in their seats and "crept out of the theater and stumbled into a cab, not knowing what to say to each other."

The public knew what to say. "Wow!" "Let's see more of the kid who gets killed off!" "How do you spell a long, low whistle?" And "Who's the babe in the sweater?," read the preview cards. The fan letters which poured in after the national release constantly referred to "the girl in the sweater." She was too new for audiences to know her name, so studio publicity agents dubbed Turner "The Sweater Girl," promoting her to the public with this typical starlet nickname . . . a nickname Turner came to hate.

After *They Won't Forget*, Turner was borrowed by Samuel Goldwyn for a small part in his lavish production, *Adventures of Marco Polo* (1938), starring Gary Cooper and Sigrid Gurie, Goldwyn's exotic "Norwegian" discovery who turned out to be from Brooklyn. Goldwyn obviously had seen *They Won't Forget*, as Turner was cast as a ripe young

SWEATER GIRL

handmaiden eyed by warrior chieftain Alan Hale (although his wife, Binnie Barnes, has her own eyes on the situation). Wearing an alluring black Oriental wig and a dress with maximum cleavage, Turner delivers a handful of lines in her distinctive, soft voice. She plays in two short scenes with Hale, and it is obvious that both the director and the producer felt her main talent was in her full bosom. The film was a landmark in Turner's career, however, as her eyebrows were shaved off for the role—and never grew back. (Both the film and her role were unworthy of the sacrifice of two such beautiful brows.)

Next Turner returned to Warners for a small part in an unjustly neglected little treasure, *The Great Garrick* (1937), produced and directed by James Whale and "personally supervised by Mervyn LeRoy." Set in 1750 and elegantly designed by Anton Grot, *The Great Garrick* is a witty and graceful film involving a plot to discredit the great English actor David Garrick by the Company of the Comédie Francaise (who mistakenly think he has insulted their ability.) An excellent cast includes Brian Aherne as Garrick and Olivia de Havilland as the perfect damsel in distress, making a magnificent entrance wreathed in furs and frowns, begging to be rescued.

Lana Turner, listed next to last in *The Great Garrick* credits, has a tiny role as one of a trio of chambermaids who giggle and curtsy and provide a Restoration lustiness to the story. These three, in full skirts and low necklines, are like a Huey, Louie, and Dewey of the bawdy wench tradition. (In addition to Turner, one of the maids is played by Marie Wilson.) Turner is a sweet-faced and dark-haired young beauty with spirit and humor, but practically no lines. She manages to remain utterly in character, however, and her billing indicates her status as LeRoy's personal protégé, as such a minor role normally would receive no screen credit.

Lana Turner is often listed next as having appeared in *Four's A Crowd* (1938), a screwball comedy in which Errol Flynn, Rosalind Russell, Olivia de Havilland, and Patric Knowles play two sets of bickering lovers who change and rechange partners. However, careful screening of this film reveals no sight of Turner, even in the crowd scenes. ("If she's in it," says one fan, "she must be under the table.")

At this point (1938) Lana Turner was eighteen years old and steadily earning $75 a week—a fortune by her standards. She was receiving good publicity from Billy Wilkerson in the *Hollywood Reporter* and was being watched over and protected professionally by Mervyn LeRoy, the closest she ever came to

THE ADVENTURES OF MARCO POLO (1938). As Nazama's maid

THE GREAT GARRICK (1937). As Auber

a real father figure. When LeRoy was lured away from Warner Brothers by Metro-Goldwyn-Mayer, he elected to take Turner with him. Jack Warner told him to go ahead. Warner felt the little starlet would never amount to anything.

LeRoy moved into MGM as King of the Lot, a highly respected director, both personally and professionally. Thus it was that Lana Turner, an inexperienced newcomer, came through the gates of prestigious MGM on the arm of an important man. She was instantly "sold" to Benny Thau, one of Metro's most important starmakers, and enrolled at the famous little red schoolhouse with fellow students (or, as they viewed it, fellow inmates) Mickey Rooney, Judy Garland, and Freddie Bartholomew.

MGM was serious about the business of shaping and molding stars. Under the careful guidance of the studio, Lana Turner now really began to learn the ropes of filmmaking, following a carefully laid out plan that would eventually lead her to stardom—if the public so decreed. Her first role at MGM was a clue to the plans they had for her. She was assigned a part in one of the Hardy family films, *Love Finds Andy Hardy* (1938).

Among the most popular films of the thirties were those featuring the homespun warmth of the Hardy family: Judge Hardy, a paragon of wisdom and fatherly virtue, his son, Andy, his wife and daughter, and the various townspeople who lived around them in dear old Carvel. As personified by Lewis Stone and Mickey Rooney, Judge Hardy and Andy came to represent the typical American father and son to the average moviegoer. Metro's plan for the series was perfect. The films cost pennies to produce and made zillions at the box office. They also provided a showcase for up-and-coming young MGM female stars. Over the years, Andy Hardy paid court to Judy Garland, Kathryn Grayson, Esther Williams, Donna Reed—and Lana Turner.

In *Love Finds Andy Hardy*, Turner was selected for the juicy role of Cynthia Potter ("that redheaded vampire"). The part was so small that it might have gone unnoticed had Turner not had such obvious on-screen presence. Whining and pouting, dimpling and winking, she teases Andy Hardy, kisses him, makes him show off for her, and generally makes the most of a juvenile femme fatale role. Even as a teen-ager, Lana Turner represented the girl who'd rather sit on the diving board to show off her figure than get wet in the water . . . the girl who'd rather kiss than kibbitz.

Lana Turner was a natural beau-

LOVE FINDS ANDY HARDY (1938). With Mickey Rooney

ty, and in this little role she exhibits an easy manner, a self-confidence beyond her years. She knew how to get attention for herself. Even when Judy Garland sang, Mickey Rooney mugged, and Lewis Stone pontificated, Lana Turner had her own way of being noticed. She wrinkled up her nose, drew her arms around her bosom in a self-hug, and emitted her delicious giggle. Even though her role had virtually disappeared from the story line by the time the big moment of Andy Hardy's heart-to-heart talk with his father came along ("Look, Dad, can I talk to you man to man?"), Cynthia Potter was not forgotten.

Lana Turner played her last bit part in *The Chaser* (1938), a film not generally listed in her filmography. Released approximately one month after *Love Finds Andy Hardy*, it was the story of a young ambulance chaser (Dennis O'Keefe) and the beautiful girl who reforms him (Ann Morriss). The film was stolen by Lewis Stone as a drunken doctor, and Turner received no billing in a cast that included Nat Pendleton, Henry O'Neill, John Qualen, and Irving Bacon. (A 1933 version of the story was called *The Nuisance*.)

Another small role awaited Turner in her next film, *Rich Man, Poor Girl* (1938), a forgotten movie which starred Robert Young and Ruth Hussey. The story? A rich man falls in love with a poor girl, or if details are necessary, a very wealthy young fellow falls in love with his own secretary. She is unwilling to accept his advances, although she loves him too, because she is afraid he won't understand her eccentric family. So the young man arrives incognito to board with the family and look them over. This *You Can't Take It With You* rip-off was pleasant enough, earning good reviews. Bosley Crowther in *The New York Times* called it a "genial and heart-warming little comedy which crackles and pops so pleasantly that you can hardly hear its joints creak." Young and Hussey are charming in the leads, and Lew Ayres received recognition for his portrait of a wild-haired, radical nephew. As the daughter of the family, Turner had a small role but looked lovely and handled her dialogue well. The film did nothing for her career, but it didn't hurt her either.

The same was true for her next, *Dramatic School* (1938), a low-budget version of *Stage Door*, illogically set in a decidedly non-Parisian Paris (presumably to ac-

RICH MAN, POOR GIRL (1938). With Guy Kibbee

commodate the exotic accent of its leading lady, Luise Rainer.) The plot concerns Rainer's deep urge to succeed as an actress. She plays a little waif who works all night in a factory to pay for her lessons at the dramatic school—a familiar Rainer *schtick*.

Despite its programmer status, *Dramatic School* is lavishly produced in the MGM tradition, and follows that studio's habit of featuring young players with star potential to see if the public notices them or not. Among these hopefuls are Ann Rutherford, Virginia Grey, and Lana Turner. (Paulette God-dard has co-star billing with Rainer, but her part is small.)

Turner is cast as a wise-cracking student—the sort of role that Ginger Rogers played in Warners musicals like *42nd Street* and *Gold Diggers of 1933*. Turner is remarkably at ease among such capable performers as Rainer, Henry Stephenson, and Gale Sondergaard (as an aging actress-turned-teacher who is jealous of Rainer's talent). She speaks her few lines well, registers a distinct presence, and looks adorable.

At this stage, Lana Turner is still all dimples, curly hair and high

DRAMATIC SCHOOL (1938). With Virginia Grey and Paulette Goddard

school charm, more of a cheer-leader than a Cleopatra. The idea of her as a serious dramatic school student is a bit far-fetched. She is exceptionally pretty, but not yet glamorous—the kind of girl every boy in school might want to take to the Senior Prom, provided it wouldn't worry his mother too much.

There are moments when *Dramatic School* looks as if it might turn into a great screwball comedy. (Rand Brooks, as the no-talent son of Henry Stephenson, the school's director, matter-of-factly tells Ann Rutherford: "I have no talent. My father just told me.") But Luise Rainer is not about to let any dramatic moment get away from her, and the film remains serious.

Turner's apprenticeship continued with another role in one of MGM's popular series films. *Calling Dr. Kildare* (1939) was the third entry in the series based on a group of characters created by Max Brand. Like the Andy Hardy series, the Kildare films were used to showcase new talent that Metro hoped to build into box office draws. Turner was now given the first of her really meaty roles as a grown-up sex object, and she played it to the hilt.

Set at the fictional Blair Hospital, the Kildare films concerned the testy but affectionate father/son relationship between the noble Dr. Kildare (well-played by Lew Ayres) and the cranky old Dr. Gillespie. Lionel Barrymore—in a wheelchair because of his arthritic condition—played Gillespie as a cripple who hid his affections behind a gruff exterior. ("I know why none of his patients ever die," suggests one nurse. "They're afraid to.") Barrymore wheels around yelling "get out of my way, stupid" and "you congenital idiot" at his staff—all of whom love him for it.

When Dr. Kildare is sent to work in a slum clinic to gain experience, he meets Lana Turner, playing the sister of a gunshot victim that he treats illegally. (Kildare's performing a blood transfusion in a slum basement, using his own blood, is a feat that ought to qualify him for the Nobel Prize in medicine.) Heavily made up in a cheap but glamorous style, Turner is lovely underneath the pancake. Her self-confidence in her sexual magnetism is apparent. Lighting a cigarette for Kildare and handing it to him, she casually stops her car in Central Park and seduces him. When Kildare compliments her on the beauty of her name (Rosalie), she informs him sarcastically, "Well, it ought to be pretty. I paid $5 for it."

It is clear in *Calling Dr. Kildare* that MGM had become aware that it may have something in Miss Turner—she's not just another in-

CALLING DR. KILDARE (1939). With Lionel Barrymore and Lew Ayres

génue. Beautiful closeups linger over her face. This time, for the first time, she's no cheerleader. She looks believable as the ripest young floozie on the block. Saddled with a character that is not too well-written, she defines it with her presence (something she would have to do often in her long career). Her essence is so distinctive that when Lew Ayres goes home to Mom and tells her he's going to marry Turner ("Is she a nice girl, Jimmy?"), it is easy to imagine mothers all over America turning faint at the thought of a Lana Turner with furs, high heels, and jangling bracelets, waiting in the wings to grab their wholesome sons.

Turner's character is one she will repeat ... a luxury-loving bad girl who is not really all that bad. ("I love a cold wind whipping around a skyscraper—with a sable coat to keep me warm," she tells Ayres.) Barrymore offers Ayres some fatherly advice on girls like Turner: "She's a bad little girl and you should have known it ... Books could be written about Rosalie."

THESE GLAMOUR GIRLS (1939). With Lew Ayres

Even as a kid, Lana Turner could create *that* kind of character and make it believable. In a well-played final scene with Barrymore, the young actress holds her own against the old pro as she breaks down, cries, and admits she'll have to start all over again to make something of herself. ("Well, you're young," pontificates Barrymore.)

It was now 1939. Technically, Lana Turner was still a starlet, but she was considered attractive enough and popular enough to carry a programmer as its leading lady. From this point on, until her big break, she was the official star name of each film she made. The first of these films, *These Glamour Girls*, included in its title the one word which defined Turner's image for years to come. "Glamour" became a byword for Lana Turner.

These Glamour Girls has an impressive line-up of budding female talent, as befits the studio that had "more stars than there are in the heavens." All were being tried out before the public in this entertaining film, a silly story enlivened by good pace, elegant decor, beautiful clothes—and that line-up of pretty young starlets. Lovely Jane Bryan, with her intelligent quality, plays a rich girl whose family has lost its money. Ann Rutherford is a bubble-brain, and Anita Louise is a beautiful villainess. In a sad subplot, Marsha Hunt plays an "older girl" who has been coming down to

DANCING CO-ED (1939). With Ann Rutherford, Roscoe Karns, Leon Errol, and Lee Bowman

college weekends for five years. She ends up parking her car in front of an on-rushing train and calmly applying lipstick while she awaits oblivion. (Talk about glamour.)

Turner herself is well-cast as a dance hall girl mistakenly invited down to Kingsford College by a drunken and cynical college boy (Lew Ayres—too old for the role). Turner is on the brink of understanding her own sex appeal, halfway between being a bouncing teenager and a grown-up destroyer. Whereas make-up had supplied some of her maturity in *Calling Dr. Kildare*, here she generates it for herself.

Turner triumphs over the stuffy, rich crowd ("champagne for breakfast and two-timing for lunch") by honestly admitting she's a taxi dancer. With a gleam in her eye, she invites the boys to pay her to dance with them. In no time, she's surrounded by a flock of admirers. Dressed in slinky black while the other girls wear full skirts and puffed sleeves, Turner is a knockout as she takes the floor for an impromptu dance that is the highlight of her sweater girl years.

TWO GIRLS ON BROADWAY (1940). With George Murphy

Easy and relaxed, full of life, naturally graceful, Lana Turner had warmth and a sense of fun that readily communicated itself to audiences. When she flashes a smile of delight at her dance partner, it is a perfect film moment to show what made her a star.

MGM had only the dimmest notion of what the world of debutantes, college boys, and bids for weekend house parties was really like. They turned the situation into a steaming cauldron of thwarted love affairs and crossed-up matings. The audience is able to sort out the right boy and the right girl within the first ten minutes. Unfortunately, it takes the script writer longer, although there are some good lines. One deb's mother refers to her daughter's date, a boy from Pittsburgh, as "that awful nobody from the Middle West." And a fellow taxi dancer offers Turner this advice: "There's only one way to make a college boy look up to you—climb a ladder." *These Glamour Girls* also contains a visually stunning sequence with duplicated mirror images in a fun house, not unlike Orson Welles's ending to *The Lady From Shanghai.* But its main visual accomplishment is red-headed Lana Turner.

Next was *Dancing Co-Ed*, one of those college films of the late thirties which starred young women like Turner and Betty Grable (neither of whom had been within a false eyelash of a college campus) as typical American college girls.

Dancing Co-Ed tells a flimsy tale about a movie company searching for an actress to play a co-ed in an up-and-coming film. They decide to plant Turner at a midwestern university and "discover" her. Turner falls in love with the editor of the campus newspaper (Richard Carlson), who is outraged when he learns of the plot but relents when Turner flashes her dimples at him. "Miss Turner wears abbreviated dancing togs with what seems almost like originality; that is the important thing to remember about *Dancing Co-Ed*," said *The New York Times.*

Actually, there was nothing important to remember about *Dancing Co-Ed.* It would have passed into oblivion had it not been the place where Lana Turner met bandleader Artie Shaw, the man who would become the first of her husbands. (He played himself in the film.) According to later reports, Miss Turner and Mr. Shaw took an instant dislike to one another. (They should have trusted their instincts.) They spent the entire production sitting at opposite ends of the set, although cynics said Turner did this for her own protection because crew members, who hated Shaw and his temperament, were planning how to drop a sun arc on his head without hitting the blonde beauty they adored.*

Two more films awaited Turner before she officially broke out of the starlet mold: *Two Girls On Broadway* and *We Who Are Young* (both 1940). The first co-starred her with Joan Blondell in a re-hash of *The Broadway Melody*'s plot. Two sisters come to Broadway to make the big time in show business and fall in love with the same guy. Each one spends most of the running time sweetly trying to give him up in favor of the other one. The film is weak, but it does afford Lana Turner a big production number with George Murphy, in which her natural gift for dancing was put to good use.

We Who Are Young teamed her with John Shelton in a story written by Dalton Trumbo (who should have known better), about a young couple who marry on a wave of optimism and face bitter times when they both lose their jobs. It's only a matter of minutes before their furniture is repossessed. It seems, however, like a matter of hours before a rich old benefactor comes along to rescue the husband from his ditch-digging job and Turner from the prospect of giving birth in a charity ward. Lana Turner plays

* Turner was always popular with film crews and most co-workers. Her reputation as a reliable professional is solid.

a sweet young thing and keeps her chin up—not easy to do with a script like this. It was a Depression story which had grown old hat by 1940.

Turner had now been at MGM two years, and she had kept active with a series of low-budget films that either afforded her a lead in a weak picture or a meaty small role in a somewhat stronger script. She had worked hard and performed well, and no one could deny her natural looks and ability. Her distinctive vocal quality, combined with her obvious physical characteristics, marked her for stardom. She was cooperative, too, and willingly posed for stills and accepted any role offered.

Metro bosses had kept their eyes on her (no doubt that's *exactly* what they did.) Their question was: could she handle a big part in an "A" production? They decided to give her a chance, and she was cast in the role that lifted her out of the starlet category and up into the ranks of star. And at MGM, that *did* mean *star*. As production began and progressed, it became evident to all concerned—in particular the director, Robert Z. Leonard—that Lana Turner could handle such a role. Her part was expanded, and her future was ensured.

The film was *Ziegfeld Girl* (1941), and in it Turner was billed fourth after James Stewart, Judy

WE WHO ARE YOUNG (1940). With John Shelton

ZIEGFELD GIRL (1941). With James Stewart

Garland, and Hedy Lamarr (in that order). Its all-star cast required a big-time publicity budget, a large portion of which went to promoting Lana Turner. ("The public will soon see Lana Turner in the best role of the biggest picture to be released by the industry's biggest company within the next few months.")

By this time, Lana Turner was becoming known in private life as "the night club queen." She was young. She was beautiful. She liked to have a good time. She already had her first marriage and divorce behind her (Artie Shaw). At age 21, she was no longer a kid in anyone's eyes, including her own. *Ziegfeld Girl* marked the beginning of what would become typical in Lana Turner's film roles. It meshed what the public knew was going on in her private life with the fictional role she played on film. Sheila Regan, Turner's character, likes to go to night clubs and have a good time, not unlike the off-screen Lana herself.

Ziegfeld Girl tells the story of three young girls who become stars—or is that human chandeliers—for the Ziegfeld Follies. The three are Judy Garland, a non-glamorous daughter of an ex-vaudeville star; Hedy Lamarr, the exotically beautiful wife of an out-of-work concert violinist; and Lana Turner, in a tailor-made role of an elevator operator who's as wise to the world as she is ambitious. At first, she's a nice kid from a happy Irish family, planning to marry her devoted boyfriend (James Stewart). After she joins the Follies, her head is turned by fame and easy money. Soon she's all set up in a fancy apartment, with satin sheets on the bed, "*bonne nuit*" embroidered on her pillow cases, and the most expensive perfume to be had sprayed in the air.

Ziegfeld Girl confirms the idea of Lana Turner as the ultimate in glamour. She sits in a bubble bath wearing a diamond and emerald necklace and an ornate headdress. She tosses a mink coat on the floor and walks over it. She throws a leopard coat over her elevator operator's uniform, and makes us believe in *both* costumes. She's still young enough and kittenish enough to be a kid running an elevator, but she's also knowing enough and sensual enough to look good in a leopard coat. With *Ziegfeld Girl*, Lana Turner became the embodiment of what Hollywood stood for in its golden years.

Ziegfeld Girl is overly long and stuffed with multiple plots. The storyline is slowed down (but made tolerable) by Busby Berkeley's delightfully insane musical numbers. The stars parade in costumes loaded with gauze and tulle, shiny fringe and tiny rhinestone stars,

ZIEGFELD GIRL (1941). As Sheila Regan

ZIEGFELD GIRL (1941). With Hedy Lamarr and Philip Dorn

faces appropriately frozen, while Tony Martin sings "You Stepped Out of a Dream." It is a fascinating film to see today for a survey of talents—those that will last and those that won't. Judy Garland made it by virtue of talent wedded to looks, and Lana Turner made it with looks wedded to talent. Hedy Lamarr, perhaps the ultimate in beauty, had no vitality to bring to her role and thus couldn't last despite her looks. ("She looks better all wrapped up than the rest of them do all unwrapped," observes a stage hand.) Tony Martin and the teen-aged Jackie Cooper, in small parts, never clicked in films, but James Stewart and even Dan Dailey (in a very small

role) had presence and went on to greater stardom.

Lana Turner played her first truly demanding role, and played it well. She looks tough and wise one moment, and innocent and appealing the next. She makes dialogue like "I'm two people . . . neither one of them any good" sound better than it has any right to sound. Above all, she pulls off the film's biggest dramatic moment in fine style. Once again, Lana Turner made a long walk on film. As a show girl who is down and out, sick and desperate, she attends the opening of the new Ziegfeld Follies—a show she would have been in had she not ruined her life. Forgotten now, she sits alone in the

46

balcony, but illness forces her to leave. Out in the lobby, she starts down the stairs just as *her* music floats out ... "You Stepped Out Of A Dream." Pulling herself together like an old soldier hearing a battle cry, Turner walks slowly, regally down the stairs, trailing her fur behind her, every inch the showgirl, until she suddenly collapses and tumbles down the stairs to her death. One big moment like this is enough to clinch any career. And Lana Turner knew it.

In *They Won't Forget*, she walked into the chance to become a movie star. In *Ziegfeld Girl*, she walked into a lifetime of superstardom. Whenever her chance came, Lana Turner squared her magnificent shoulders and stepped right out. Whatever the moment, whatever the disaster, whatever the applause, or lack of it, she rose to the occasion and gave the public the glamour and excitement it expected. She always went on ... a definition of the word "star."

With *Ziegfeld Girl*, Lana Turner stepped out of a movie dream and into a real-life dream as a movie star, with a $1500 per week salary to prove it. *Life* magazine did two major layouts on her within less than eight weeks, and her fan mail was booming. Next up was another big budget picture opposite one of the most popular and respected actors in the business, Spencer Tracy. The film was to be a remake of the durable property, Robert Louis Stevenson's *Dr. Jekyll and Mr. Hyde*.

According to reliable sources, Turner was originally supposed to play the role taken by Ingrid Bergman. The parts were reversed at the last minute when Bergman asked for and got the better role of Ivy, the barmaid. Bergman definitely knew what she was doing, as she steals the film with her sexy portrait. ("I know what's what. You have to, if you're a barmaid.") Magnificently photographed by Joseph Ruttenberg, radiant with the glow of robust health, Bergman is at the peak of her beauty. Her sensuous use of her arms and legs and her discreet frankness in bedroom scenes with Tracy are remarkable. She brings all her talent to the role.

Lana Turner, on the other hand, is badly miscast as the young Victorian ingénue. Like Joan Crawford, Turner had a modern quality

GLAMOUR GIRL

which always seemed slightly out of place in a period drama (although she wore the costumes well). The first sight of her in *Dr. Jekyll and Mr. Hyde* (1941)—holding a hymn book and singing in a church pew—shows a full-lipped beauty who is ogling Spencer Tracy in a most un-Victorian manner. At an impressive scene at a dinner party, she looks almost like a naughty child trying to behave well for company.

The script of *Dr. Jekyll and Mr. Hyde* is the familiar tale modernized by way of Freudian psychology. Some of the dialogue is inadvertently silly. Donald Crisp, playing Turner's father, objects to Tracy's romancing her in public: "Good heavens! Nibbling your knuckles!" Turner responds to this with one of her trademarks—a gleeful giggle. The script tries to provide a sense of period with lines such as "Has anyone read that poem by the new chap—Oscar Wilde?," and a sense of horror with familiar genre lines like "after all—separating the facets of the brain—rather ambitious, isn't it?"

The film has a slack pace, largely due to the familiarity of the storyline. Tracy, as always, gives an expert performance. (He has one splendidly ridiculous dream in which he whips two horses that turn

In the early forties

into Ingrid Bergman and Lana Turner!) Although the character transformations are done with make-up, Tracy creates a subtle personality change as well, letting Jekyll's compassion become Hyde's lust.

For a young lady who had suddenly become a big star and hot property, *Dr. Jekyll and Mr. Hyde* was a disappointment. Turner's role was small, and she had almost nothing to do except sit at dinner tables or in opera boxes, saying "I'm worried." Furthermore, the balance of the plot is thrown off by her presence. The ingénue is supposed to exude purity, and Turner has a carnal quality despite her youth. Although she looks incredibly lovely, Lana Turner is not the type to be found at the harpsichord with roses in her hair and forgiveness in her heart. Her acting is adequate, even touching and heartfelt in moments, seeming to come from a wellspring of genuine feeling. But the plain truth is that she's wrong for the part.

Dr. Jekyll and Mr. Hyde, however, fared well at the box office and Lana Turner reaped the benefits of having co-starred in a handsome, lavish production in which foggy streets and damp pavements were juxtaposed with stunning costumes and handsomely dressed sets.

Her next film was also a period piece, but it was modern and irreverent in attitude and therefore right for Turner. *Honky Tonk* (1941) paired her with the star she was meant to be paired with—Clark Gable, whose image was that of a soft-hearted womanizer with a tough exterior, just the sort of man who would know what to do with a Lana Turner.

Dedicated to the confidence man, the "often unsung but seldom unhung hero of the Old West," *Honky Tonk* gets off to a rousing start with Clark Gable neatly slicking out of a prospective tarring and feathering and leaping on a train, where he meets Turner. She's so ruffled and ribboned he mistakes her for a fancy lady, so she suckers him out of $10—which she donates to the Salvation Army. When they arrive in Yellow Creek, Nevada, Turner is asked by her father (Frank Morgan): "Did this fellow bother you?" She smugly replies, "Not half as much as I bothered him."

Although ostensibly a Western, *Honky Tonk* is played on a sound stage against painted backdrops. It is more a typical MGM glossy drama than anything else, and like most of those, it runs a bit too long. Its story rambles through a labyrinth of plot complications involving Gable's rise to power as a political manipulator, his marriage to Turner, the loss of their expected baby, his exposure to the

DR. JEKYLL AND MR. HYDE (1941). With Spencer Tracy

townspeople as a crook ("a man with clean hands in a country where honest men work"), and the couple's ultimate reconciliation. A strong cast provides solid support: Claire Trevor in one of her bad-girl-with-heart-of-gold portraits; Frank Morgan as Turner's drunken father; Marjorie Main as a plain-talking landlady; and Albert Dekker as a crooked sheriff.

Lana Turner is given royal treatment, not only in having the King for her co-star, but in constant references to her physical charms. "This room looks like you," Gable says to her, "Everything in the right place." And "you're prettier than a little white kitten with a blue ribbon on it."

Although *Honky Tonk* purports to be about empire building, it really is about only one thing: sex. The exchanges between the two stars are loaded with double meaning. (The censor must have been out to lunch.) Gable, flashing one of his famous leers, gives Turner advice on how to take her bath, "Why don't you jump right in and get wet all over? You'd feel better." And when she tells him, "I'm going to

HONKY TONK (1941).
As Elizabeth Cotton

have respect from you," he winks and laughs, "That ain't why you married me, honey." Even the title, *Honky Tonk*, suggested to audiences plenty of non-Victorian sex.

The film confirmed that Turner was a real star, and not a one-shot flash-in-the-box-office. She moved right into the frame with Gable and made the picture as much hers as his. She's still a little girl who has to fall back on a bustle and a pout in their big scenes together, but she *can* hold her own by whatever means. Gable, the man with "a

streak of good, and a streak of mean" and Turner, wearing black corsets, diamonds in her hair, and black lace stockings (parading in front of him like a proud little circus pony), are a terrific team.

When Gable breaks down Turner's locked door on their wedding night, she has one of her most glorious moments. A look of childlike delight flashes over her face, full of virgin expectation and excitement. Later, she wakes up in bed, luxuriating like Scarlett O'Hara. But where Vivien Leigh was a desirable woman who could

HONKY TONK (1941). With Clark Gable

act and who happened to be cast opposite Clark Gable, Turner was Lana Turner. When she wakes up, she makes the audience think not only of what he did for her—but what she must have done for him!

In addition to all the sex and glamour, Turner had a big dramatic scene in *Honky Tonk*, in which she is ill and broken after the loss of her baby. MGM felt she was capable of handling it (and she was), but the scene also represented their bow to something they had begun to sense in her nature. Turner had a disturbing quality, and it grew stronger as her career progressed. Her next film brought it out in the open.

Johnny Eager (1941), in which Turner was co-starred with Robert Taylor, used the violent nature of her sexual magnetism to advantage. MGM hit the American public with a lurid advertising campaign. "T-N-T," screamed the ads. "TURNER N' TAYLOR ... they're dynamite in JOHNNY EAGER, the flaming drama of a high-born beauty who blindly loved the most icy-hearted Big Shot gangland ever knew." The film itself didn't quite deliver all *that*, but it did deliver Turner a strong dramatic role. She made the most of it, or, considering the weakness of the script, she made the best of it.

Johnny Eager has dialogue that keeps late night show addicts rolling on the floor. For instance, a villain bursts into Robert Taylor's apartment, tries desperately to kill him in a rough-and-tumble tussle, and is finally shot by Lana Turner. Following this high drama, Robert Taylor jumps to his feet, smooths his hair, straightens his tie, and comments casually, "I wonder what was eating him!"

The story concerns a big-time crook, out on parole and allegedly going straight, who is instead masterminding a dog-racing track and continuing his illicit operations. As a front, he pretends to be a taxi driver living in a shabby apartment. His parole officer brings two young sociology students to this setting—and when one of these girls turns out to be Lana Turner, no one is more surprised than the audience. Dressed up in platform heels, a huge purse, and a bizarre hat, Turner is a highly unlikely student of anything outside the sound stages of Hollywood.

Taylor and Turner are instantly attracted to each other, but she turns out to be the adopted daughter of his arch political enemy (Edward Arnold). Arnold hates Taylor, feels he is incapable of reforming. ("You can't change your habits any more than a weasel can stop sucking chicken blood.") A convoluted plot has Taylor framing Turner, Turner nearly going mad, Taylor redeeming himself by

JOHNNY EAGER (1941). As Lisbeth Bard

JOHNNY EAGER (1941). With Robert Taylor

freeing her from his love, and his ultimate death, shot down in the streets in the crime-does-not-pay film tradition.

Meandering all over, the story-line includes a subplot about Taylor's friendship with a drunken lawyer, superbly played by Van Heflin, who won an Oscar as best supporting actor. *Johnny Eager* is poorly paced and poorly written—but it has one asset in addition to Heflin—Lana Turner. She is on the screen a minimum of time, but her presence haunts the scenes in which she does not appear. Every time a door opens, the audience hopes she will enter, so they can have another look at her, swathed in mink from head to toe, her blonde hair spread over the fur in masses of curls. Turner tackles her scenes of desperation and near-madness with all she's got. She makes up in emotional intensity what she lacks in technical skill.

The box office success of Clark Gable and Lana Turner in *Honky Tonk* convinced MGM to reteam them, this time in a modern story, *Somewhere I'll Find You* (1942). (One reviewer pointed out Metro had discovered that "Gable is to Turner as flint is to steel.") The two stars play newspaper reporters, falling in love and quarreling all over the world: New York, Indo-China, Manila, and finally (with a patriotic finish) on Bataan. Once again, Gable plays the man women want to be seduced by, the roving-eyed soldier of fortune. Turner plays a girl originally engaged to his brother (Robert Sterling) who falls over as soon as she sees him. "To heck with maidenly modesty," she cries. "Confidence is what a girl needs." In *Somewhere I'll Find You*, Turner displayed plenty of confidence, whether she was ferrying Chinese children to safety or clinching with Gable while the bombs fell. The film itself was no bomb, however, and did well at the box office.

Lana Turner was so firmly established as a star that MGM next used her as one of the "guest stars" in a film about young autograph hunters. *The Youngest Profession* (1943) starred Virginia Weidler, Edward Arnold, and John Carroll. Turner appeared along with Greer Garson, Walter Pidgeon, Robert Taylor and William Powell as one of the stars the youngsters track

SOMEWHERE I'LL FIND YOU (1942). With Clark Gable

SLIGHTLY DANGEROUS (1943). With Robert Young

down to acquire that holiest of grails—The MGM Star Autograph.

Off-screen Turner's natural good humor and sense of fun were well known. The qualities had always been present in all her characterizations, and MGM decided to capitalize on them by putting her into a comedy. *Slightly Dangerous* (1943), her next film, is a pleasant picture in which her performance can best be described as delicious. This time she's behind the soda fountain instead of in front of it, playing a soda jerk in Hotchkiss Falls, New York who has just won $2.50 worth of merchandise for coming to work on time every morning for 1000 days. (Another 1500 punctual mornings and she gets $10.00 worth of merchandise.)

Turner's character, Peggy Evans, is bitter. She makes a speech about how the gods played a trick on her when she was born: "Now let's make this one a nobody. No home. No family. Nothing." (Someone in the script department had evidently been over at Warners watch-

DU BARRY WAS A LADY (1943). With Red Skelton

ing old John Garfield movies.) Out of boredom, Turner bets she can do the job blindfolded, and she dishes up plenty of banana splits before her new boss (Robert Young) fires her. She then decides to skip town, making it look as if she were a suicide. In New York City she spends her life savings ($150) on a new look, although when she walks out in her new clothes and new hairdo, she looks more like $1,000,000 than $150.

The story complications include a bucket of paint, which hits her on the head, feigned amnesia, an adoption by a crotchety old millionaire (Walter Brennan), who thinks she's his long-lost daughter, and her inevitable tangle with Robert Young, who comes looking for her. Naturally, he finds her. They fall in love, giving Young an opportunity to utter one of the most memorable romantic speeches ever directed at Lana Turner: "I couldn't hate you, darling, not even if you turned out to be a female impersonator. And I bet my bottom dollar, you're not."

Slightly Dangerous has a good cast. Turner herself is delightful. In a scene with Young at a restaurant, she does an improvisational dance that is completely captivating. Brennan is good as the old crank, and Dame May Whitty and Eugene Pallette lend support as a nanny and newspaper tycoon, respectively. Alan Mowbray, in a tiny role

as a drunken opera-goer, steals the show when he praises Robert Young after Young's nearly disastrous fall out of a balcony seat: "Hate music. Love acrobats."

"Lana Turner" now meant "Hollywood glamour." Her name soon began to appear in other movies as a symbol for beauty and sophistication. In Danny Kaye's *Wonder Man* (1945), a girl on a park bench justifies her looks by saying, "Some people think I look just like Lana Turner." In *Without Reservations* (1946), directed by her former mentor, Mervyn LeRoy, her name is mentioned so often it's as if she owned the picture. ("Lana Turner? That's a glandular attraction," says one character.)

Anticipating this fame, MGM had her make a little joke appearance in *DuBarry Was A Lady* (1943), starring Gene Kelly, Lucille Ball, and Red Skelton. Gene Kelly inspects a line-up of chorus girls with a super-critical eye, and the last one in line is Lana Turner. Kelly's double take made a pleasant surprise that caused audiences to burst into applause.

Turner was now powerful enough at the box office not to need Clark Gable or Spencer Tracy or Robert Taylor—or even Robert Young —as a co-star. Her next picture was hers and hers alone, and its title called attention to that fact as well

MARRIAGE IS A PRIVATE AFFAIR (1944). As Theo

as providing her first solo billing. *Marriage Is A Private Affair* (1944) was made and released at the peak of publicity over her tangled marital relations with her second husband, Steve Crane. Their marriage/annulment/remarriage headlines were much in the news, generating more plot complications and excitement than the picture itself.

Marriage Is A Private Affair, based on a novel by Judith Kelly, is the story of a wartime marriage. As the bride starts down the aisle, she has a momentary panic because she can't remember the groom's name. (She's only known him three days.) Their union undergoes stresses and strains when Theo, the young society belle, finds marriage and the motherhood which follows to be a

limited existence—temporarily. For a few moments it looks as if the film will be an early women's liberation document, as Turner asks herself, "Does marriage mean I have to give up everything? That Theo is dead? I don't feel different." But Turner and her husband (John Hodiak) are reunited via short-wave army radio hook-up from her apartment to his New Guinea flying base. The other man (James Craig) understands—after all, it's all for the war effort.

Marriage Is A Private Affair reflects wartime morality, and is interesting sociologically if not cinematically. Turner had never been more stylish on film, wearing more than thirty Irene-designed costumes. Even the aprons, gushed

MARRIAGE IS A PRIVATE AFFAIR (1944). With John Hodiak

the publicity, were designed by Irene! Critics all commented on Turner's looks, but most made jokes of the plot. Her line to her one-month-old baby was singled out for ridicule: "Oh, Tommy, please grow up and learn what it's all about . . . so you can tell me."

Wartime ambience also dominated her next film. *Keep Your Powder Dry* (1945) was the story of three girls who join the Women's Army Corps: Turner, a night club habitué who joins for a lark; Laraine Day, a general's daughter who respects the Corps; and Susan Peters, a humble soldier's wife whose motives are all love and patriotism. Turner and Day feud all through basic training, while Peters stands on the sidelines, sweetly acting as referee. The film's ending finds all three arm-in-arm, commissioned as officers, and ready to lick the Axis forces. Reviews were scathing, with *The New York Times* suggesting that the writers had dashed off the script "on the doorstep of the studio beauty shop." Turner's personal reviews—as had become routine—referred only to how beautiful she looked.

An updated remake of *Grand Hotel* followed, a patriotic mishmash called *Weekend At The Waldorf* (1945). A reference is even made to the 1932 film in the new dialogue. When Walter Pidgeon, caught in Ginger Rogers' hotel room, quotes one of John Barrymore's speeches, Rogers comments, "Why, that's right out of *Grand Hotel*." "Yes," replies Pidgeon wryly, "and we're off to see the Wizard." This exchange proves that, contrary to what people think, MGM did have some sense of humor about itself.

Weekend At The Waldorf is a slow, talky film. The interlocking pieces of the story fail to fit together, and fall all over the floor like so much confetti. The script is awful. Walter Pidgeon plays a character named Chip Collyer, affording Rogers the opportunity to say, "Goodbye Mr. Chip . . . Collyer" not once but twice. The cast, however, is excellent. Ginger Rogers plays Irene Malvern, a movie star who is bored with life, but not by her wardrobe. In one scene, she wears a hairdo like an Italian sausage with a gold hoop hanging out of it. It is to Rogers' credit that on her it looks good. Walter Pidgeon is perfect as the weary war correspondent who falls in love with Rogers, and Van Johnson is good as a young flyer with a piece of shrapnel near his heart (an update of the Lionel Barrymore character from the original).

The all-star cast includes Keenan Wynn as a cub reporter; Phyllis Thaxter as the bride-to-be of a Kansas doctor; Robert Benchley as

KEEP YOUR POWDER DRY (1945). With Agnes Moorehead

a cranky hotel dweller whose dog is about to have pups; Edward Arnold as a villainous director of a phony oil company; and even Xavier Cugat in the Wedgewood Room, dishing out sambas and malapropisms while huge production numbers swamp the story line. The production is MGM lavish, with people reflected in mirrors, standing around amidst expensive furniture, wearing gorgeous clothes, and attending cocktail parties where cardboard hors d'oeuvres abound and where ginger ale flows like wine.

For this film, Lana Turner was assigned the role of the young public stenographer, the part originally taken by Joan Crawford.

The part has been considerably cleaned up for the wartime remake. Crawford's Flaemmchen (which she played brilliantly) was a convincing girl of the streets, out for what she could get and grabbing it with both hands. Turner's girl from Tenth Avenue is attractively played, but the hard reality of Crawford's portrait is gone. Turner appears to be just too luscious to have suffered!

Many people have pointed out that a more obvious casting for *Weekend At The Waldorf* would have been a role reversal between Turner and Rogers. Rogers could have been wisecracking and realistic as the stenographer, common in that lovely way she perfected.

WEEKEND AT THE WALDORF (1945). With Van Johnson

WEEKEND AT THE WALDORF (1945). As Bunny Smith

Rogers ended up looking static and overdressed in her part, while Turner had to play down her looks and figure in order to be believable as a secretary.

However, as Turner expert Lou Valentino has pointed out, Irene Malvern is supposed to be world-weary, a star of many years. Turner is too young for this role, and Rogers does play it well. Turner, as always, is lovely to look at, particularly when she visits the Star-lite Room in a white sequined strapless gown. She is every inch a star, and nothing can hide it as she shines at the ringside table. Some secretary!

Turner's next film is arguably her most famous role. The Postman Always Rings Twice (1946) gave her the part which best mixed her sex appeal with the violence it seemed inexplicably linked to, and let her penchant for tragedy express itself fully.

Turner's career did not abound in great films, but it did abound in great screen moments. Her walks in They Won't Forget and Ziegfeld Girl, her mad scene in Johnny Eager, her execution in The Three Musketeers, among others. Her first entrance in The Postman Always Rings Twice is among these scenes. The searching camera follows her dropped lipstick as it rolls across the floor, over to her white, open-toed high heels and up her perfectly proportioned figure to her insolent face framed in a white turban. This image of the tanned and beautiful Lana Turner, dressed in white shorts and halter top, is one of the most famous in American pin-up history. When she applies her lipstick, preening herself in front of John Garfield merely to show him plenty of what it is he can't have, an entire generation remembered the image.

Based on James M. Cain's novel, Postman tells the story of an itinerant drifter (Garfield), a character halfway between the out-of-work rebel of the thirties and the I-won't-work rebel of the fifties. He arrives via hitchhiking at The Twin Oaks ("Chicken Dinner—$1.25") where a MAN WANTED sign and a sizzling hamburger take on an unmistakable sexual significance. After Garfield meets Turner (wife of the owner, played by Cecil Kellaway), every word is loaded with meaning from that point on. "You won't find anything cheap around here," Turner warns Garfield, after he looks her over. "The harder the wind blows, the hotter it gets," he replies. After their first kiss, she takes out her compact and cleans up her mussed lipstick and carefully, deliberately reapplies it after looking at him, as if to say, "So what else is new, fella?"

The Postman Always Rings Twice is loaded with hot, repressed sex. Everything that happens in the film depends on Turner and Garfield being able to generate that feeling. They can and do. When they play the juke box and dance on a hot summer night, the Latin music in the shadowed room lit by a neon sign makes anything—including murder—seem not only possible but downright necessary.

The link between sex and violence which is now associated with Turner's private life makes *Postman* an even more disturbing film today. In a stunning scene in Garfield's room, she lures him to murder her husband with a closeup that is an image of Satan as a beautiful woman, electric with evil. Eyebrows arched with tension, mouth half-parted, voice whispering, Turner is overlaid with a silvery magnetism that shocks. Entirely gone now is that kittenish girl of her early career.

The tangled web *Postman*'s lovers weave leads them to murder, to jail, and ultimately to hate and distrust. When they finally sort out their conflicting emotions, the final irony occurs. Turner is killed in an automobile accident, with Garfield driving. The last we see of her is her dead hand, once again dropping the lipstick tube through which we first met her.

In *Postman*, Garfield goes to his death in the gas chamber, saying death is "like you're expecting a letter. You're afraid you won't hear him ring . . . but he always rings twice." Turner and Garfield rang more than twice with their torrid relationship in this film.

Next Turner went into *Green Dolphin Street* (1947), a beautifully mounted film. Set in the 1800's on an island in the English Channel, it is a *Gone With The Wind* epic: big, sprawling, and telling so many stories at once that the audience is exhausted as well as entertained. Lana Turner and Donna Reed play sisters Marianne and Marguerite, like a beautiful Tweedledum and Tweedledee ("Bless my soul if they aren't a pretty pair of fish!," comments one observer.) Turner's character (Marianne) is a modern girl, bold, scheming, determined to take over the family shipping business and even, by her own admission, "not quite nice."

Both girls fall in love with the same man, Richard Hart, an interesting actor who played only four major roles in films before his untimely death at thirty-five. By a series of plot complications, Hart ends up in New Zealand, where he sends for Donna Reed, the sister he truly loves, to join him as his wife. However—and the audience is asked to swallow this—he can never get their names straight and sends for the wrong one! When Lana Turner arrives, he marries her anyway, and poor Reed enters a

THE POSTMAN ALWAYS RINGS TWICE (1946).
With Cecil Kellaway

THE POSTMAN ALWAYS RINGS TWICE (1946).
With John Garfield

GREEN DOLPHIN STREET (1947). With Edmund Gwenn

convent. (She's well out of it.)

Green Dolphin Street contains enough events to fill five movies: an earthquake (in which Lana gives birth), a tidal wave, a native uprising, and a flood. The big earthquake sequence features trees uprooting and crashing on native heads, geysers gushing, earth cracking, opening and swallowing people—and Lana screeching her head off in childbirth. "It's the worst disaster in New Zealand history," comments a survivor. One of the worst in special effects history, too.

Turner is exquisitely gowned in the film, and handles her histrionics with ease. She is now a thorough professional, as adept at crying as she is at smiling, as believable portraying a tragic figure as she is at looking beautiful. If a faint tinge of the mechanical creeps into her performance from time to time, it is no more than the script deserves.

More excitement was generated off-screen during *Green Dolphin Street* than on. During the filming, Turner made headlines when she suspended production to fly to Mexico to visit her current love, Tyrone Power (who was filming *Captain From Castile* on location). Everyone, including Turner, expected the beautiful couple to wed, but, in one of life's ironies, they did

GREEN DOLPHIN STREET (1947). With Richard Hart

not. Instead, Power ended up marrying an unknown actress who was currently playing a bit part in *Green Dolphin Street* as Lana Turner's maid! Linda Christian, one of the people waiting on the set while Lana and Ty kept their rendezvous, later turned the tables when Power romanced her in Europe while Turner cooled *her* heels back in Hollywood.

Next up was a film version of Sinclair Lewis's second-rate novel, *Cass Timberlane* (1947), with Turner reunited with Spencer Tracy. The story concerns a May/December romance between a girl from the wrong side of the tracks and an influential judge. Both Tracy and Turner improve upon the original Lewis characters, making them warmer, more

human, and certainly more likable. Although seemingly an odd couple, Tracy and Turner are lovely together. They have a good deal of fun with Turner collapsing in giggles when Tracy tickles her . . . and with his appreciatively eyeing her when she wears a tight pair of jeans.

The story concerns the problems their marriage faces when Cass's friends won't accept his new wife. After the loss of their baby, the social strictures of their small Minnesota town confine her too much, and she is tempted by the bright lights of New York and the winning ways of Cass's best friend (Zachary Scott). When Scott takes the small town girl on a whirlwind tour of the big city, she is particularly thrilled to see Walter

CASS TIMBERLANE (1947). With Spencer Tracy

HOMECOMING (1948). With Clark Gable

Pidgeon at a classy party. (This was a typical Metro stunt—tossing a real-life star into the movie, like casually dropping a $1000 poker chip.) Things are happily resolved, however, with Turner breathing "You're the only consistent thing, Cass, in this whole cockeyed world" in Tracy's ear.

Homecoming (1948), Lana Turner's next film, paired her with Clark Gable for the third time. A mature and touching film, it is a story about the adjustments married couples had to make to separation during World War II. Gable plays a society doctor to whom a country club dance is more important than a slum dwelling project. Anne Baxter is that familiar soap opera creature, the doctor's wife, wearing fur and pearls and standing nobly by the cocktail shaker, keeping the chintz curtains fresh while he fights the war. Turner's role is a down-to-earth nurse with a crusading spirit, a decidedly deglamorized role with no wardrobe but a pair of battle fatigues. She is assigned to Gable as his chief nurse in combat, and the two gradually fall in love after first hating each other. Her courage and dedication set an example for the doctor, whose life is changed through knowing her.

HOMECOMING (1948).
As Lt. Jane "Snapshot" McCall

Homecoming was meant to be a modern version of the Ulysses story, and Ulysses is Gable's character name. (Turner translates it into "Useless," which becomes a shared joke between them.) Back home waits his Penelope, the wife played by Baxter, her hand being held by Gable's best friend (John Hodiak).

The old Turner/Gable magic is still present, only now the situation between them is totally equal. Turner is no longer the little girl flirting deliciously with the big male star. Now she is Lana Turner, his equal in star magnitude and sexual magnetism. The post-war Gable was an older looking, sadder-faced man, but he is warmed up and teased by the laughing Turner, who is still easy and natural in front of the cameras. She was the right kind of fun-loving companion for the King. In a scene in which they go out to bathe in a Roman ruin, he's shy and she's bold, a good reversal of their former screen selves. In a scene redolent of wartime democracy, the director (Turner's old friend, Mervyn LeRoy) plays two of America's biggest sex symbols for laughs, treating them like human beings, real people instead of movie stars.

Homecoming is a tender love story of human growth and mature love. Gable's own loss of his wife seems to have heightened his un-

THE THREE MUSKETEERS (1948). As Milady DeWinter

THE THREE MUSKETEERS (1948). With June Allyson

derstanding of his character's feelings when Turner dies at film's end. Once again laid out in a death bed, Turner, who could always look vulnerable when she wanted to, played her final scene for simplicity, creating a touching end for a story of a love that goes unfulfilled.

As a change of pace, Turner next was cast in a lavish costume drama, based on Dumas's *The Three Musketeers*. Except for her brief guest appearance in *DuBarry Was A Lady*, it was her first Technicolor film. Fans turned out in droves to see their girl in living color—a sight

well worth waiting for. As Milady DeWinter, Turner was covered with jewels and costumed exquisitely. The drama of her first appearance on screen is heightened by the effect of having her sit in a darkened carriage, giving the audience a sense of an apparition beyond life, a mysterious creature in the dark. When Turner finally *does* lean slowly forward into the light—and the Technicolor—audiences were not jerked out of their mood and back to earth. She *was* unreal. A proper goddess.

The Three Musketeers has its

best moments in a duel performed and literally danced in a park setting. Splendid camera work follows Gene Kelly, (who, as D'Artagnan, proves he could flash a sword and twirl a cape with the best of 'em) as he leaps and dashes and defeats Richelieu's men. A big name cast included, besides Kelly, Van Heflin, Vincent Price, Angela Lansbury, Keenan Wynn, Gig Young, Robert Coote, and June Allyson as D'Artagnan's true love, Constance. ("I'm just a girl who works at the palace.")

Turner does full justice to the juicy role of a truly evil woman. ("Beware of strange men, dark roads, and lonely places. That woman will destroy you.") Once again, she is glamour personified as she leans toward Kelly and breathes, "Whatever my reputation, I assure you, my D'Artagnan, I don't take love lightly." Whether gloriously costumed or without make-up as a prisoner, Turner is magnificent. In a final scene, she gets the baroque justice she deserves at the hands of an executioner. Wearing vivid green with purple veils, while the wind machine pumps away and colored lights flash, Turner takes another

A LIFE OF HER OWN (1950). As Lily James

A LIFE OF HER OWN (1950).
With Ray Milland

MR. IMPERIUM (1951). With Ezio Pinza

of those long walks for which she is so famous. She gives *Three Musketeers* a little much-needed life by way of her own death scene.

At this stage in her career, Turner was somewhat indifferent to film-making. She had initially gone on suspension over her role as Milady in *The Three Musketeers*, refusing to play in the lavish costume drama. Studio pressure had convinced her to cooperate, however, although Louis B. Mayer was said to be almost wishing he were rid of her, despite her obvious box office draw. The reason for this uncharacteristic Mayer conflict was Turner's private life. In addition to her many romantic escapades, she had garnered more headlines in a sensational affair with much-married millionaire, Bob Topping,

who became her third husband following completion of *Musketeers*. Obviously not needing money, Turner took the first vacation from work she had known since she was barely sixteen years old. She was off the screen for a period of time, returning partly out of boredom, partly out of studio pressure . . . and partly, it was said, out of disillusionment with her latest marriage.

Turner's next film, panned at the time and even disowned by its director, George Cukor, is an unexpectedly mature story. *A Life Of Her Own* (1950) both uses the conventions of the woman's film and works against them, letting darkness and despair settle over its plot like a great blight. As model Lily James, Turner creates a character riddled with anxiety. She is that familiar women's picture character, the girl who gets out of a small town to make it big in the city. ("I won't be back," she tells the cab driver, as she boards the train back in Kansas in the film's opening scene.)

By virtue of hard work and determination—not to mention the looks of a Lana Turner—Lily James makes it to the top of the modelling profession in the cat-eat-cat world of New York. She is no starry-eyed kid, and she has no interest in romance: "I've had men buzzing around me since I was fourteen years old. I want to be somebody. All I have is myself and how I look.

I'll work hard."

Although she likes being on her own, when Lily James reaches the top and takes a look around, she feels lonely. When she meets married man Ray Milland (owner of a copper mine), they begin an affair. At first the relationship provides the audience with the typical idyllic interludes in the country, "their" song, "their" place, and "their" undying devotion. But in the soap opera tradition, Milland's wife is a cripple and he just *can't* leave her, especially when he was the one driving the car when . . . etc. In an ending totally untypical of the genre, Turner pulls herself together, rejects a con-

THE MERRY WIDOW (1952). With Una Merkel

templated suicide and tells Milland: "I don't think I can live without you, but I'm going to." She walks out on him, a free woman. After one dream of a career as a replacement for romance disappoints her—and another dream of romance itself lets her down—she is free to live a life of her own.

Beautifully directed by George Cukor, *A Life Of Her Own* contains an excellent performance by Turner. She is perfectly cast as a woman who reaches the top of a profession in which "you don't really *do* anything . . . people just use you." It is a film which deserves re-evaluation, particularly in times of heightened awareness of the woman's role in films and society.

A Life Of Her Own showed the public a slightly more mature-looking Lana Turner. Still beautiful and looking younger than her years, Turner nevertheless had to face the problems of Hollywood's impending collapse in the early fifties. MGM began to wonder what to do with her. She was a top star, and a big box office attraction, yet *A Life Of Her Own* had not fared well financially. Perhaps she should make a different type of film, go in another direction.

Another direction resulted in a candidate for Turner's worst film while under contract at MGM, a farce called *Mr. Imperium* (1951).

Although Turner did not sing, she danced fairly well, so Metro decided to turn her into a musical comedy star. After all, she had made a musical while a starlet (*Two Girls On Broadway*) and her big star-making hit was a semi-musical (*Ziegfeld Girl*). Planning a Technicolor escapist musical, Metro decided to cast Turner with Ezio Pinza, the singer who had made a romantic splash in Broadway's *South Pacific*. The man who thought up the romantic team of Turner and Pinza is probably the same one who thought of mixing pickles with ice cream. It is impossible to believe for one minute that a girl like Lana Turner would go for this musical version of Edward Everett Horton. Pinza is downright silly as he barges up to her and introduces himself as Prince Alexis ("Just call me Al.")

The story is an old chestnut about a king who loves a chorus girl, only the chorus girl becomes a world-famous movie star. They reunite years later at a dude ranch in a romantic interlude before they must return to their various responsibilities. (Being a movie star is, after all, a lot like being royalty.) Hope for pleasant comedy is introduced at the dude ranch in the persons of Marjorie Main and Debbie Reynolds, but any real comedy relief is purely accidental. For instance, when Turner asks Pinza, the

THE MERRY WIDOW (1952). With Fernando Lamas

King, "What does your son want to be when he grows up?" Or when Pinza appears wearing western garb—spaghetti with chili sauce.

The only thing worth mentioning in *Mr. Imperium* is the music, and there's not much of that. Pinza sings beautifully an Italian song, "Andiamo" (while he and Turner bump along in a mule cart) and the beautiful "Solamente Una Vez" while she sparkles in the moonlight. Turner herself does one number (dubbed), "My Love and My Mule."

Before *Mr. Imperium* could ruin her forever, Lana Turner made a musical film that was, whatever its imperfections, far superior to the Pinza film. MGM's 1952 version of the durable *Merry Widow* is the Neiman-Marcus of film musicals. It is stuffed full of expensive furniture, gold-trimmed uniforms, sterling silver place settings, ostrich-feathered costumes, and jewelled knick-knacks. It is as if the audience has been gathered

THE BAD AND THE BEAUTIFUL (1952). With Gilbert Roland

together because they are all shockingly wealthy—and this will be a shopping tour of Europe to end all shopping tours of Europe.

This version of *The Merry Widow*, starring Lana Turner and the handsome Fernando Lamas, was not like the von Stroheim version with its decadence and sense of European rot. Nor was it like the 1934 version directed by Ernst Lubitsch and starring Jeanette MacDonald and Maurice Chevalier. *That* film was all bubbles and wit, as sophisticated and subtle as only Lubitsch can be. But although this version may not

be vintage champagne, it isn't beer either. More of a good red, with plenty of body and a good pedigree.

Turner and Lamas embody the ultimate in physical beauty à la Hollywood. She is stunning in Technicolor, and he, especially in tight pants, is the perfect Latin lover; not *too* oily and not *too* pretty, but handsome enough and smooth enough to fit the role of dream-prince. Although as a pair they lacked the humorous self-awareness of MacDonald and Chevalier, Turner and Lamas made the characters their own. By shifting the emphasis of the story, they

THE BAD AND THE BEAUTIFUL (1952). With Kirk Douglas

LATIN LOVERS (1953). With Ricardo Montalban

created a sense of passion and frustrated love, which is what their version of the old property is all about. The casting of Lamas best illustrates this difference between the 1952 *Merry Widow* and the Lubitsch film; it is more Latin than French. It is therefore no less beautiful, but just a trifle less amusing, less sophisticated. To compensate, it has its own charms: stunning decor, Turner looking magnificent, a funny Una Merkel (who had also appeared in the thirties film) and a nasal Richard Haydn in a good character role.

Although some people feel Lana Turner's version of *The Merry Widow* is more fizzle than fizz, in terms of beauty of production, it is excellent. Visions of the dancers at Maxim's, gorgeous in scarlet and brilliant black . . . and the pink, white, and gold of the waltzers in a spectacular final number, linger in a viewer's memory. The public turned the film into a semi-hit, although critics joked that, since Turner had announced her intentions to divorce Topping, the title should have been *The Merry Grass Widow*.

Turner's next film performance might be called the best she ever gave. It was the film that MGM was built to make and Vincente Minnelli was meant to direct. It might even be the role that Lana Turner was born to play . . . that of movie star Georgia Lorrison in *The Bad And The Beautiful* (1952). Turner was given top billing in an impressive cast that included Kirk Douglas, Dick Powell, Walter Pidgeon, Barry Sullivan, Gloria Grahame, and Gilbert Roland. The public's idea of the private Lana Turner in 1952 was that of a spoiled glamour girl with an excess of beauty and an excessive love life. Audiences believed in Turner as Lorrison. In addition, the part itself, loosely based on Diana Barrymore, was one Turner could give everything she had to—and did.

Georgia is a lush with one foot in the gutter when she meets Jonathan Shields (Kirk Douglas), a Hollywood hustler who has gate-crashed and gambled his way into picture power. Georgia is the kind of girl who is willing to sleep with Shields just because it's 4 A.M. and she wants to turn the light out. However, he sees her potential: "When you're on the screen, no matter how bad you are, no one looks at anyone but you." He molds her into a star, after first dumping her fully clothed into his swimming pool, a Hollywood ritual baptism. He learns that the way to control her and inspire her is to make love to her. After she's a success, he loses interest in her, having finished his work, as it were.

The Bad And The Beautiful is

superbly directed by Minnelli, a man who *knows* Hollywood. He recreates atmosphere—a typical Hollywood party, a sneak preview, shots of hundreds of different types of staircases stored in a studio warehouse, a two-bit agent who breaks down and weeps when his client lands a job, and a fast-talking sharpie who rents leopard costumes. ("Plenty of fright. You'll need to add shoulder pads, of course.")

Turner's biggest scenes come when, at the peak of her success, she goes to Douglas's house, only to find him already entertaining another girl—upstairs. The girl is played by sexy starlet Elaine Stewart, who effectively delivers the line "there are no great men . . . there's only men." (Stewart, sexy though she is, could never take Lana Turner's place. Significantly, while Turner is still a star, Stewart works as a hostess on a television quiz show.) Confronting Douglas, Turner wisely underplays, while he chews the scenery. She gives all she has in the scene which follows*—one of the most famous on film. Rushing away from Douglas's mansion, she drives off in her car at top speed. As her speed increases, her hysteria mounts until, blinded by tears and auto lights (a mockery of the klieg lights she had so desperately desired), she crashes her car and collapses in tears.

Lana Turner is excellent in *The Bad And The Beautiful*. For once a glamorous movie star is played by one. She understands the role, and she makes it hers. None of the sex symbols who have been touted as actresses—not Hayworth or Gardner or Taylor or Monroe—have ever given such a fine performance. Yet she was not even nominated for an Oscar.

Despite her success in *The Bad And The Beautiful* as a dramatic actress, MGM persisted in its plan to make Turner into a musical comedy star. Her next, *Latin Lovers* (1953), was supposed to be a light comedy with a little music—a dollop of whipped cream atop a fizzy soda. What resulted was more like a Bromo Seltzer, with no relief in sight.

Turner plays a big business tycoon who secretly sees a psychiatrist: "Oh, Dr. Newman, I'm so mixed up." Do they like her for herself or for her $37 million? (Only a girl who looks like Lana Turner can make that a viable question.) To reassure herself, she has become engaged to John Lund, who plays a character with $47 million. Still riddled with doubts, she decides to go to Brazil to think it over. In Brazil, she is told, the men know what they want when they see it.

* This scene was added after the film's production had been completed.

THE FLAME AND THE FLESH (1954). With Carlos Thompson

BETRAYED (1954). With Clark Gable

"There's something in the air." There's something in the air, all right.

When Turner meets Ricardo Montalban, they fall madly in love, but must suffer through the scenario before they can live happily ever after. *Latin Lovers* is a piffle in which the major action takes place in the wardrobe department. Turner changes clothes every five minutes. But not even the beautiful clothes and the Latin music—or the sight of Lana doing a fetching samba with Montalban—can turn this pumpkin into a golden coach.

Several major Hollywood stars (Gene Kelly, among others) were now going overseas to make films and take advantage of a new American tax law. The studios, too, were interested in filming in Europe, both for the box office draw of location shooting and to use their own frozen foreign funds in film production. Turner joined the parade of big-name stars who made films overseas, first to Naples for *The Flame and the Flesh,* and then to Holland and England for *Betrayed.* Accompanying her on this sojourn was the handsome actor who would become her next husband, Lex Barker. ("We're just good friends," said Lana and Lex as they departed California.)

The Flame and the Flesh (1954) gave fans a brunette Lana Turner in

THE PRODIGAL (1955). With Edmund Purdom

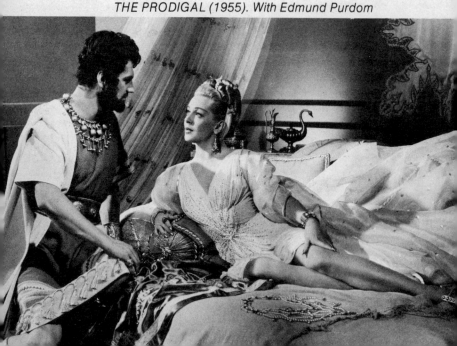

THE PRODIGAL (1955). As Samarra

a film which attempted to capture the lustiness of the foreign films then flooding the United States movie houses and providing formidable competition for the Hollywood product. *The Flame and the Flesh* was shot largely in Naples, and its authentic footage was the best part of the film. Armchair travellers were not yet so glutted with the sight of location work in films that they could not respond positively to the beautiful sights of Naples. *The Flame and the Flesh* is about a girl of the streets who moves in to share an apartment with an old friend. His other roommate is Carlos Thompson, a singer of Neapolitan street songs by trade and a trifler with women's affections by hobby. This character is supposed to be engaged to Pier Angeli, the trusting daughter of a local cafe owner. But when Thompson and Turner look over each other's flesh, the flames rise. They run off together, but Turner soon realizes it won't work. "Faithfulness is not one of your great virtues," he sneers at her. "Or yours, either," she snaps back. Turner finally walks off into the night, teetering on her high heels, making a noble sacrifice for Angeli's happiness. Very little believable passion was generated by this talky film which featured no action and lots of lines like "I'm crazy when I'm with you and crazy without you" and "Why is it that I love you but don't like you?"

Turner was then reunited with her popular co-star, Clark Gable, for the fourth—and last—time in her next film, *Betrayed* (1954). The main betrayal is that of the screenplay, which badly lets down its two durable stars. Set in 1943, the plot involves a Dutch Intelligence Officer (Gable) with a woman recruited as a spy by his department (Turner). The movie gets off to a splendid start in a mysterious house set over a labyrinth of steel corridors containing radio apparatus at which spies are clicking away to signal Gable. Dressed as a peasant, he is driving an innocent-looking vegetable cart in the streets of Amsterdam, tapping out Morse code with his foot. After an exciting capture, he is rescued in true Rover Boy style by a guerrilla band headed by Victor Mature.

From that moment on, however, the film dies. Turner and Gable seem tired, unable to generate their former sexual magnetism. Although she has not aged since *Homecoming*, he definitely has. They look at each other with dull eyes, their former secret twinkles and sense of mutual fun depleted. He's no longer the tomcat on the prowl, and she's not the cute kid with the kittenish qualities. Alas, they don't even seem to be Clark

Gable and Lana Turner. They look like two people who just want to get it over with, put their feet up, and have a cup of coffee.

Betrayed is stolen by Victor Mature, that underrated actor of maximum flamboyance who did so much to inject humor and life into so many dying films. Playing the dashing guerrilla leader who blows up bridges, kills Germans, and generally has a high old time of it, before he is revealed as a villainous traitor, Mature delivers what might stand as the definitive line regarding his own film career: "I'm in this strictly for laughs."

Next for Turner was one of those films that inspire critics to think they are comedians. *The Prodigal* is ready-made for the one-line put-down, and Turner's role is one of the silliest in film history.

It was the fate of most Hollywood sex symbols to eventually be cast as a goddess. Rita Hayworth played Terpsichore and Ava Gardner played Venus—but these roles were in light musical comedies. Turner was saddled with playing the High Priestess of Astarte back in old Damascus (700 B.C.) in a script that thought it was for real. It can only be to Turner's professional credit that, knowing the film was a joke, she suited up in her goddess

THE SEA CHASE (1955). With John Wayne

beads and walked through her role, giving the film all her glamour but none of her talent.

Her entrance is another one of her great movie walks. To the jangle of pagan music, she appears from behind a gaudy curtain and, with torches in her hands, undulates around a claustrophobic tent wearing baubles, bangles, and beads. "She is not a follower of Jehovah," hisses a witness, by way of explanation.

The design of *The Prodigal* gives the impression of various departments struggling with how to create the world of 700 B.C.—and forgetting to communicate with each other. Turner is dressed like a kooch dancer, and Louis Calhern, as the Grand Factotum of the Temple, is dressed like a Victorian lampshade. Turner and the little girl she is training to take her place as High Priestess wear matching outfits—Mother-Daughter costumes for goddesses.

The script writers have strung together a list of lines from other Biblical epics and let it go at that. "She's in my blood," says Edmund Purdom, in the title role. "I can never belong to any one man," says Turner. "I belong to—*all* men." "She's what every blind man sees," observes one slave to another.

Watching Lana Turner clack across a marble floor in modern high heels . . . and seeing her move among "her people" like a movie star among her fans . . . audiences can't help but wonder. Casting a star like Turner this way must have seemed like a great idea to someone, but what about *her*? How did she feel when, having proved she could act, she was only assigned roles like this? As film historian Douglas Lemza has pointed out, *The Prodigal* is something not even Carol Burnett could parody. This sort of nonsense requires a Cecil B. DeMille to keep it moving.

For all its idiocy, *The Prodigal* nevertheless silences laughter at the awful moment when Lana Turner, as the ultimate sex goddess, is pelted with rotten vegetables and stones by the populace. She is bewildered and hurt, having believed "her people" will always love her. With a sudden movement, she jumps from a high tower into a flaming cauldron below, a human sacrifice to those who have raised her up to where she is, but who will no longer care for her. No movie star needs a scene like that.

MGM had always had a bankable property in their golden girl, Lana Turner. Not once since Mervyn LeRoy first brought her through the gates had they ever loaned her to another studio. Turner was not only a box office draw, but she was reliable and professional. Now, with financial pressures starting to mount up and with Turner's films not doing as well as usual, Metro made a deal for Turner's services, loaning her out twice. She was to make *The Sea Chase* for Warners and *The Rains of Ranchipur* at Twentieth Century-Fox.

The Sea Chase (1955) teamed her for the first time with John Wayne. Toe to toe, they were equals in star magnitude. Head to head, they were not as well matched, as tiny Turner (even in her highest heels) barely grazed the big Duke's shoulder. Turner plays a shady lady who has been spying for the Germans in Australia at the outbreak of World War II. Wayne plays a German freighter captain whose loyalties lie with the old regime and not with the Nazis. (The audience has to do a bit of mental reorganization to accept Wayne as a German. Although it is disconcerting to hear him bellow out "auf-weeeee-der-zane," Wayne knows, as always, what he is doing. He plays the German captain as if he were a noble cavalryman, loyal to his military past. In other words,

THE RAINS OF RANCHIPUR (1955). With Richard Burton

DIANE (1955). With Roger Moore

he's a good American German.)

When Wayne sneaks his boat out of Sydney harbor to bring his crew home to Germany, Turner is smuggled aboard before she can be caught as a spy. They are pursued by a British ship, on which one of the officers is Wayne's closest friend. The old freighter makes an heroic voyage, although unknown to Wayne, one of his Nazi crew members murders some innocent men while ashore for supplies.

Lana Turner is swathed in mink once again, blonde and blue-eyed in color, sporting red-red lipstick and nail polish. She is sleek and glamorized to the teeth. Wearing a low-cut, clinging gown as she stands in the doorway of Wayne's quarters, her face wears a look of here - we - two - stars - are - to-gether - at - last, or, better yet, she seems to be saying, "Me Turner. You Wayne."

The two stars perform well, but there's no real chemistry between them. Wayne is a rugged, out-of-doors hero, and Turner is the ultimate in indoor girls. An audience can practically smell her expensive perfume. Together in the frame, they look like a bad splice job, seeming to come from two different movies.

The sprawling story of *The Sea Chase* might have been better if directed by John Ford or Howard Hawks. As it is, an ominous note is sounded by villain Lyle Bettger when he intones, "We're going to be a long time on this ship ... a long, dreary time." With an overly long running time and too many plot angles, all the tension goes out of the story line. Lana Turner has very little to do. She stands around, changing her clothes often, and polishing her diamonds. (When the ship runs out of fuel, no one realized that there is enough carbon in her jewel case to sail them right down the main street of Berlin.)

Turner didn't fare much better at Fox with *The Rains of Ranchipur* (1955). A remake of *The Rains Came* (1939) in color and wide screen, *Ranchipur* afforded Turner some lovely costume changes. Her character is a selfish and decadent woman, miserably married to Michael Rennie. He has married her for her money, and she has married him for his title. They have lived a series of disenchanted evenings together ever since.

The two have come to Ranchipur to purchase horses ("We can put up at the Palace.") While there, they encounter an old friend of Turner's (played by Fred MacMurray) as well as Richard Burton in the role originally created by Tyrone Power, that of a dedicated Indian doctor. Burton, in skirts and turban, tries to be sexy in this "wisdom of the East" role, but fails. He has no real glamour, no exotic al-

Lana Turner in 1955

lure like Power. In his romantic scenes with Turner, there is no heat on his part, only on hers.

The Rains of Ranchipur tells a soap opera story. Despite the use of location footage (mixed with interiors) and the special effects of the earthquake and flood, the film is sluggish. It has predictable dramatic moments. Turner is frightened by the inevitable cobra into Burton's arms, and her bad girl character turns out to be misunderstood: "Has it ever occurred to you that I might be lonely?"

Following these loan-outs, Turner returned to Metro to make her last picture under contract to the studio at which she had grown up. *Diane* (1955) was a costume picture based on the life of the Countess de Breze, the infamous Diane de Poitiers.

Diane has sumptuous settings and costumes. There is wealth in every tiny detail. A fruit bowl in the shape of a black swan. Handsome carved screens. Lovely tapestries. Oranges hollowed out into little baskets and filled with strawberries. And, of course, Turner, wearing so much fur that she's practically an ecological disaster.

A clumsy screenplay which strives for literacy nearly swamps Turner. But the elegance, the polish she had acquired in her years at Metro enable her to pull herself—and the rest of the cast—through the film. The part of Diane is one of those cleavage-and-catastrophe roles for which her regal carriage is perfect. By the end of her sojourn at Metro, Turner is no longer an elevator girl who wants to wear mink. She may be Queen of the Gypsies—but she is a Queen.

The reaction to *Diane* was not good. The time for this sort of lavish woman's picture had passed, and Lana Turner faced a major career crisis. After over eighteen years as a top money-maker (her films had grossed over $50 million), her contract was to be dropped. In February, 1956, shortly after her 36th birthday, Lana Turner left MGM. The little girl had grown up and was being kicked out of the big nest she had helped to feather. How did Lana Turner feel? Was she frightened or was she worried?

With characteristic good humor, Lana flashed a smile and gave out her optimistic philosophy: "I am quite sure that around the corner is something good . . ." Around Lana Turner's corner was something named Johnny Stompanato . . .

By the end of 1937, Julia Jean Mildred Frances Turner had become Lana Turner. By the end of 1973, Lana Turner had become Lana Turner Shaw Crane Topping Barker May Eaton Dante. And therein, as they say, lies a tale.

Lana Turner was not the first movie star to create romantic scandals. The difference for her was that she was never officially excused for her peccadilloes. She just lived through them, and finally lived long enough to have lived them down. Ingrid Bergman was ostracized—even denounced in Congress—when she bore Roberto Rossellini's child. But she was publicly forgiven and welcomed home with open arms that held an Oscar in each fist. Marilyn Monroe, when her sins were revealed, was said to be a product of her wretched past, more victim than victimizer. Ava Gardner, whose high living made international headlines, was called a modern playgirl and cited as a liberated woman who used men as men had once used her. Elizabeth Taylor Hilton Wilding Todd Fisher Burton Burton was said to be too beautiful to be responsible for anything . . . and besides, she was sickly. Lana Turner, however, suffered both scandal *and* humiliation. She was made to pay.

She started young. Even in Hollywood, a girl like Lana was un-

MARRIAGE: NEVER A PRIVATE AFFAIR

usual. As soon as she began making films, the men started flocking around her. She was rumored to be in love with this one, dating that one, breaking up with another one, about to marry or not marry a succession of eligible (and some not so eligible) men.

She got off to a flashy start in the marital sweepstakes: a late-night elopement at the end of her first date with a controversial character. Actually, Lana Turner had met Artie Shaw, her first husband, when they co-starred in *Dancing Co-Ed*, but in true Hollywood plot fashion, she hated him. She allegedly told reporters, "I never saw a man like him before. He was the most egotistical thing! He hogged the camera and he spent more time with the hairdresser and the make-up man than any actor on the lot." The next thing she knew, she was on an airplane to Las Vegas with him, to become his third wife. The four months and seventeen days of their publicity-ridden marriage were referred to forever after by Lana as "my college education."

Along the way to becoming one of the most married stars of them all, Lana Turner piled up so many lurid headlines that only an un-

100

With first husband Artie Shaw

*With second husband Steve Crane
and daughter Cheryl*

motional library index can tell her story without sensation. At the time of her marriage to Shaw, she was too unimportant to rate a *New York Times* Index entry all her own. Under the name TURNER, L., the instructions read, See SHAW, A. The entries were short and sweet, and told the whole story.

SHAW, A.: Marries L. Turner 2/14/40

Wife Sues for Divorce 7/4/40

Wife (L. Turner) Gets Divorce 9/14/40

After this unexpected marriage and divorce—swift even by Hollywood standards—Turner became known as a playgirl. *Liberty* magazine claimed that between her first and second marriages she "dated, conservatively, some 150 members of the opposite sex, was engaged to marry five different men, and actually was on the verge of going to the altar with a dozen."

Less than two years after her divorce from Shaw, Turner met a handsome young man at a night club. Before she had known him long—some sources say a month, some say nine days, but Turner herself claims four months—she had eloped with him. It was back to Las Vegas to the same justice of the peace who had wed her to Shaw and who allegedly greeted her with a cheery, "Welcome back, Lana!"

No one knew much about Steve Crane, not even Lana. It was first reported he was a Chicago stockbroker. Then it was said he was a rich tobacco heir, or a Hollywood actor on-the-make, and finally a young Los Angeles businessman. Turner said afterwards that she didn't know what Crane did for a living, and she didn't care: "I married him without thought, and even if I had pondered for a long time, for ten or fifteen minutes even, I'd have married him anyway." To her it didn't matter if he were a tobacco heir or a cigar store Indian. When Lana Turner was in love, details were unimportant. Which turned out to be just as well when Steve Crane was finally found out to be a young man from Crawfordsville, Indiana who had at that time what might be termed limited prospects.

TURNER, L.: Marries S. Crane 7/18/42

There was one detail which turned up later, however, and which did turn out to be important, very important. Shortly after Lana announced she was to become a mother, she learned Crane had been married before. Furthermore, his marriage had not been dissolved officially at the time he wed Lana Turner. With a baby on the way—and already quarreling with the handsome young man she had made her second husband—Lana found out she was not married!

TURNER, L.: Seeks Annul-

ment of Marriage to S. Crane
1/8/43
Gets Annulment of Marriage
to S. Crane 2/5/43
Recovering After Shock over
Crane's Attempted Suicide
2/18/43
Announces Remarriage to S.
Crane 4/6/43
Baby Daughter Born 7/26/43
Seeks Divorce 4/9/44

It has been said that, had she not been expecting a child, Lana Turner would never have remarried Steve Crane. In her eyes, their marriage was already hopeless, but under the circumstances, she felt she had little choice.

Turner's description of this second marriage is pathetic: "Six months with child, in as drab a ceremony as was ever performed, in the heat and squalor of Tijuana, I stood before a little man whose office sign said 'Legal Matters Adjusted' and again became Steve Crane's wife. We called a Mexican off the street for a peso or two and made him a witness." Like some small town high school girl in trouble, the allegedly spoiled movie star whose life was supposed to be all champagne and roses suffered the humiliation of going through with what she knew to be a hopeless deal. Crane had lied to her, and she had fallen for it. It wasn't the last time that Lana Turner would be conned into marriage by a smooth

talker, either.

As if to make matters even more dramatic, Turner's only child, Cheryl Christina Crane, was an RH negative baby who required special blood transfusions to survive. More headlines and more trauma for Lana.

Most actresses could go a lifetime on a string of publicity like this. For Turner there was still more to come. After her divorce from Crane, she was linked with a dazzling succession of famous boyfriends. (Over the years, she dated Howard Hughes, Victor Mature, Tony Martin, Robert Stack, Buddy Rich, Tommy Dorsey, Turhan Bey, Robert Hutton, and many more.) Chief among these was the handsome actor, Tyrone Power, the man who has been called the one true love in Lana's life. Turner and Power, however, were destined never to wed. Many feel the loss of his love was the turning point in Lana's life, as Power might have been a stabilizing influence.

When Lana Turner announced her intentions to marry for the third time, to millionaire Henry J. (Bob) Topping, the press rose to the occasion like barracuda to the bait. They described Lana as having been desolate after her divorce, as she had been "left with nothing but her $226,000 per year salary, a daughter named Cheryl, and half a dozen casual beaux." Turner's

With Cheryl in 1945

groom was scathingly referred to by *Life* magazine as "considered very talented by cafe society . . . because he inherited $7 million and plays a fine game of golf."

The wedding itself was thoroughly ridiculed by *Life* in a story entitled "For the Fourth and Definitely Last Time."* Turner's lifelong friend, Billy Wilkerson, acted as host for the reception and also as Topping's best man. Completely ignoring his close connection with Turner, *Life* pointed out that Wilkerson "moved in upper circles by virtue of having risen from speakeasy manager to publisher of the *Hollywood Reporter*—an expert on marriages, having engaged in five of them himself."

Despite newspaper cruelty and cynicism, the bride was starry-eyed and beautiful. Wearing champagne lace, fortified by a $30,000

*Although Topping was Turner's third husband, it was her fourth marriage.

With third husband Bob Topping

trousseau by Don Loper, standing in front of a bower covered with nine dozen gardenias with her darling Cheryl as flower girl, Turner did as she always did. She went forward confidently. "This is forever," Bob Topping was heard to remark to her. "Yes, darling," she replied.

TURNER, L.: Leaves for Europe with Husband H.J. Topping 5/6/48
Ill 6/29/48
Returns New York City from Europe 9/11/48
Parts from Husband H.J. Topping 9/11/51
Divorces H.J. Topping 12/6/52

Turner then continued her pattern of romancing handsome young men about Hollywood. Since her taste ran to Latin types, one of her most popular escorts was the dashing Argentine actor, Fernando Lamas. That relationship broke up over an argument concerning Turner's attraction to Lex Barker. After a long companionship, Turner took Barker as her next husband, and, just to make sure it would last, wed him again in a big Christmas ceremony.

TURNER, L.: Weds L. Barker 9/8/53
Reweds him 12/25/53
Seeks divorce from L. Barker 6/29/57

Considering Turner's overall marital record, her marriage to Lex Barker had been long and relatively steady—four years out of the headlines. Their break-up came at a vulnerable time for Lana. Her years with MGM had ended, leaving her a star-without-a-home for the first time in her career. She was now 37 years old, and in her marriages to Topping and Barker had suffered three miscarriages. She was forced to accept the fact that she would never have another child, and that her career, for the first time, might be in trouble.

Shortly after she separated from Barker, in the spring of 1957, she was approached by the young and aggressive operator of a gift shop in Los Angeles. He had allegedly obtained her telephone number from underworld figure Mickey Cohen. This young man, Johnny Stompanato, already had been married three times himself, and, at age 32, was a veteran hoodlum who knew his way around. Lana Turner fell for him.

On the evening of Good Friday, April 4, 1958*, Lana Turner was threatened by Johnny Stompanato. Her daughter, fearing for her mother's life, drove a butcher knife deep in Stompanato's abdomen. Stompanato was already dead when the authorities arrived.

*Dates in all cases reflect date of newspaper item.

TURNER, L.: Suitor J. Stompanato Stabbed to Death by Daughter C. Crane. Hollywood. 4/6/58

SEE ALSO MURDERS — CALIFORNIA

This scandal, one of the most sensational in Hollywood's history, forever marked Lana Turner. Combined with her shaky marital career, it made her appear to be one step out of the gutter, an image journalists did much to build up over the years. Turner's pathetic breakdown in court, when she brokenly attempted to testify on her daughter's behalf, was treated almost as a joke. At the very best, it was regarded as just another performance. *Life* magazine ran pictures of Turner's trial scenes in films (*Postman, Cass Timberlane*, and her current release, *Peyton Place*). Her testimony was called "a dramatic personal triumph far beyond anything she has achieved as an actress." Her words were referred to as a "Hollywood scenario," her sobbing as a "performance."

Time magazine referred to her as a "wanton," describing her sex life as a men's room conversation "everywhere from Sunset Boulevard to Fleet Street." Her love letters to Stompanato (pitifully childish) were published in leading newspapers, and large photos of Cheryl sitting alone at juvenile hall were spread across magazines. Every word of the testimony was printed.

"I did it to protect mother. I thought he was going to get her," said Cheryl Crane, "I wish I could cry like my mother, but I always hold things in."

"I didn't know what was happening," sobbed Lana on nationwide TV.

It was a three-ring circus of yellow journalism. Except for a few tired articles by old-time hacks like Louella Parsons and Walter Winchell, there was very little sympathy for Lana Turner. Not only was there a great deal of sensational press coverage of the murder of Johnny Stompanato and Cheryl's trial, but also of the tragic aftermath of misunderstanding and confusion both mother and daughter suffered in the following years.*

After the Stompanato trial, Lana Turner's private life was not only in a mess, but her professional life was

*What the press did not cover, however, was that Cheryl Crane grew up to be a responsible businesswoman. After a difficult period of internment in juvenile prison, and years of analysis, she matured and settled down. The press also did not cover Lana Turner's genuine anguish, nor her attempts to help Cheryl over the years. What has not been written is that mother and daughter are still friends, and that Lana Turner is fiercely proud of her only child, Cheryl Christina Crane.

At a Miami press party for MADAME X in 1966

With fourth husband Lex Barker

up for grabs. Turner reportedly suffered anxiety coupled with shame that immobilized her and left her fearful of the future. She had, after all, been the sole support of herself, her mother and her daughter since she was little more than a girl. If she couldn't work, what would they do? More important, what would *she* do? Work was all she had to turn to and was all she knew to do with herself. Would anyone in Hollywood hire her now? If they did, would the public accept her? Would she have the stamina and the guts to continue acting . . . to go on in the public eye?

"You know those little toys they have for children?" Turner once said. "The ones that bounce back when you hit them? That's me." She turned out to be right.

Lana Turner's last film for her alma mater, Metro-Goldwyn-Mayer (*Diane*) had been released in 1955. For two years prior to the Stompanato scandal, for the first time since she was a teen-ager, Lana Turner was not under a film contract. Like other former Hollywood studio players (both stars and non-stars), she faced the problem of finding work as Hollywood succumbed to the competition of television.

Producer Jerry Wald, searching for an actress with a box office name to head the cast in his planned production of *Peyton Place*, offered Turner the important role of Constance MacKenzie. MacKenzie was the mother of a teen-age daughter, and Turner's friends advised her not to start playing mother roles—it would destroy her glamour image. Turner wisely felt otherwise. She sensibly pointed out that, after all, she *was* the mother of a teen-ager and most people knew it. Besides, why should Lana Turner worry about playing a mother? She looked enough like a teen-ager herself to let would-be critics say anything they could.

The novel, *Peyton Place*, like *Forever Amber* before it, was *the* sensational bestseller of its day, packed with sex and sin at a time when such things were not available at every corner newsstand. Grace Metalious made a fortune

TWILIGHT OF THE GODDESS

with the book, which purported to tell all about the secret lives of the citizens in a small New England town. ("There ain't nobody livin' intelligently in this town—*nobody*.")

The film version of *Peyton Place* (1957) is superior to the novel. Reasonably mature and occasionally touching, it is a rambling movie but holds attention. Director Mark Robson put his skills as a former film editor to good use, building tension as scenes progress. There are warm and lovely moments: a Labor Day picnic, a high school dance where the young people form a circle in the dark to sing "Auld Lang Syne," and a touching farewell to the first Peyton Place boys to enlist in World War II. An authentic atmosphere of a small town is created. *Peyton Place*—the town where "two people talking is a conspiracy and two people meeting is an assignation"—comes to life.

Lana Turner is excellent as Constance MacKenzie. Constance is a character born in Peyton Place, but who had the drive to get out. She has allegedly returned to raise her daughter in her own home town "after her husband's death." Actually, she was an unwed mother, and the father of her child was a

PEYTON PLACE (1957). With Diane Varsi

married man. She is now living in a house in which the only man allowed is in a silver frame on the mantelpiece, a photo of the phoney father she has made up for her daughter. Wearing her hair in a tight French twist and pursing her lips, Turner represses her own native sensuality. She creates the opposite of herself, a woman who goes cold and suspicious at a moment's notice, an "all-men-are-alike" lady. She lives her lonely life running a dress shop, until the handsome high school principal thaws her out.

Turner's big scene in *Peyton Place* takes place in a courtroom, when she breaks down on the witness stand. Ironically, about the time she was breaking down on

movie screens all over America, she was breaking down in that same chair in real life. *Peyton Place* was made prior to the scandal in her private life, but was released almost simultaneously with the trial. Fascinated audiences watched Turner in *Peyton Place*, tense and weeping in the witness chair, and felt they were experiencing her private anguish, reenacted over and over again for their benefit.

Peyton Place was supposed to be about "the fifth season of the year—love—and only the wise or the lucky ones knew where to find it." On screen, Turner was one of the lucky ones. Off-screen, she had only the ignominy of the Stompanato trial. The film, however,

PEYTON PLACE (1957). With Lee Philips

Lana Turner in 1958

was a box office success. When the events of Good Friday, 1958 exploded on the American public, it became an even bigger hit. Lana Turner was nominated for a best actress award by the Academy of Motion Picture Arts and Sciences, her first and only such nomination. She lost to Joanne Woodward in *Three Faces of Eve*, but at least for once Hollywood had taken its goddess seriously in the acting department.

The brouhaha surrounding Turner, combined with the success of *Peyton Place*, encouraged distributors to hurry the two pictures she had made after the Wald production into release: *The Lady Takes a Flyer*, made for Universal, and *Another Time, Another Place*, the film she had been working on in England during the last difficult days of her affair with Stompanato.

The Lady Takes a Flyer (1958) co-starred Turner and Jeff Chandler. It is a comedy which begins with an airplane disaster—an ominous note. Chandler flies into Burbank airport with two of four engines on fire and no flaps, although he does manage to bring the B-17 in safely, which is more than he is able to do for the picture.

Turner plays a woman who ferried bombers during the war, but who wants to settle down with a reliable husband. Chandler is a fast living, flashy pilot ("like something out of Terry and the Pirates"). In spite of herself, she falls in love with him and joins him in starting a flying business. In a scene stolen from von Sternberg's *Jet Pilot*, the two pilot airplanes alongside each other while he tells her he loves her. He flies closer—she flies away. He catches up and touches his wing tip to hers, a truly modern love scene.

It is odd to see Lana Turner wearing earphones and a pilot's suit, sitting up front and clearing for take-off. She had by now become associated with roles in which she didn't *do* anything but act as a glamorous accessory. Her character has plenty of spunk, however, walking out on Chandler and leaving him to take care of the baby when she thinks he's been cheating on her. However, *The Lady Takes a Flyer* is a film Turner should have made when she was young and bubbly. Although she looks radiant and has moments of delightful naturalness, the film itself gets off the ground only when an airplane takes off.

Another Time, Another Place (1958) introduced Sean Connery to the American movie-going public. How he ever survived it is a cinematic miracle. Wearing black hair and eyebrows he must have ripped off a grizzly bear, Connery looks ridiculous. He tries to keep his dignity, but it isn't easy considering the script.

Lana Turner plays a newspaper correspondent during World War II in England. At this point in her career, she dresses herself like a star and never mind what her character might have worn. She looks magnificent, and is splendidly gowned in mink and diamonds. When she sits down with the newspaper boys at the poker table, it is clear she's no columnist. With her clothes, her beauty, and her poise, she is nothing else—and never could be—anything else but a movie star.

Connery plays a handsome BBC news commentator who falls madly in love with Turner, but forgets to tell her he's married to Glynis Johns. When his plane crashes near the war's end, Turner falls apart and spends six weeks in a nursing home. ("Grief" is the diagnosis.) The rest of the interminable story has Turner going to the little fishing village that was Connery's home, moving in with his wife and son and becoming close to Johns (who doesn't know about the affair). All the emotion in *Another Time, Another Place* is provided by the sound track. The production is so cheap that the entire budget looks like $10,000. (Without Lana's mink, it would have looked like $1.45.)

Turner herself looks beautiful, almost too beautiful. She seems unreal, as if she's been sprayed on the screen with a can of day-glo. Her make-up is perfect, but the glamour seems to be defining her where once she defined the glamour. For the first time her bubbling sense of fun (translate: her youth) seems to be gone, although that fact is nowhere visible on her face. *Peyton Place, Lady Takes a Flyer*, and *Another Time, Another Place* all went into release during Lana Turner's most sensational publicity. After the trial, when Cheryl was placed in the custody of her grandmother, Turner faced her greatest uncertainty. This was the period (for nearly a year or more) in which she hid from the press, trying to put the broken pieces of her life together, wondering if there would be anything left of her career. Ironically, ahead of her, Lana Turner had the best film she ever made in terms of financial success and cinematic excellence. This film, Douglas Sirk's *Imitation of Life*, (1959) insured Turner a solid income for life, as she owned a percent of the profits. It also totally revitalized her career.

Ross Hunter, a producer famous for furniture over form in film, signed Lana Turner to play the lead role in his remake of Claudette Colbert's thirties success, *Imitation of Life*, based on Fannie Hurst's novel. The film was to be directed

THE LADY TAKES A FLYER (1958). With Jeff Chandler

by Douglas Sirk, a man noted for turning sows' ears into silk purses. Turner plays the leading role of Lora Meredith, a woman so caught up in her life as a successful stage star that she is blind to those around her who need and love her. An ingenious updating of the old plot made the picture palatable to audiences, who turned it into the biggest box office hit in Universal's history.

Imitation of Life is a film that can operate on almost any audience level. At its most basic plot level, it is a soap opera, a traditional woman's picture that provides tears and catharsis. On the mythological level, it provides Turner fans with another of those uncanny real-life parallels, as Turner plays a mother who wants her daughter to have all the advantages she never had, but forgets to give her what she needs most: love and attention. ("I haven't been a good mother," sobs Turner to her daughter, played by Sandra Dee. "You meant to be," replies Dee.) For those who see a trip to the movies as a good escapist browse through gorgeous goods, *Imitation of Life* is stuffed with clothes, furniture, jewelry, make-up and hairdos, each one more eye-filling than the last. For the literary set, there is a strong story, and for the theatrical types, there are excellent performances.

In addition to Turner, who manages to capture all of Lora's self-love and plastic exterior without turning her into a selfish monster, there is beautiful Susan Kohner as a black girl who wants to be white and Juanita Moore as her tragic mother.

For those who respect cinema as an art form, *Imitation of Life* provides a stunning example of film-making, in which Sirk's form makes potentially banal content significant and touching. Even the credits reflect Sirk's talent. Jewels fall from the top of the frame onto black velvet. At first they seem elegant and chic, beautiful to see. But as they keep on falling—and keep on falling—they glut the frame with an excess of materialism . . . a perfect metaphor for the film's meaning. Through his sensitive direction, Sirk creates a story of people and their "individual and collective attempts to control their lives," as film historian Robert Smith has described it. Lana Turner gave her most appropriate performance in a film that most serious scholars regard as her best.

Following this success, Turner appeared as the top name in a series of handsomely produced, soap-opera films which attempted to imitate the imitation (of life) and recreate its box office success. Without Douglas Sirk, however, the films fell flat.

The first of these, *Portrait in Black* (1960), paired Turner with two-time Academy Award winner Anthony Quinn. The credits reflected a trend in Turner films—a listing for who did her jewelry as well as her gowns, furs, and hair styles. In this phase of her career, these credits were as important as anything else. Maybe even more important.

Portrait in Black is a murder mystery in which Turner and Quinn, illicit lovers, plot to kill her husband, a sick old tyrant played by Lloyd Nolan. Turner is a woman imprisoned by wealth, living in a home with an orange-carpeted staircase that could give a climber a nosebleed. Quinn is a successful doctor, the son of a Napa Valley fruit picker. Against beautiful location shooting in San Francisco (the film-maker's dream city), Turner and Quinn meet to make love and bemoan their fates. "All this lying and sneaking through side exits!," cries Turner as she throws off her mink and clasps Quinn to her bosom. "Sheila, Sheila, Sheila, Sheila," he replies.

After they have committed the murder, they begin to receive threatening notes from an unknown source who knows they did it. The pressure causes them to quarrel. It is material that could have made an exciting film—murder committed by desperate

ANOTHER TIME, ANOTHER PLACE (1958).
With Sean Connery

ANOTHER TIME, ANOTHER PLACE (1958). With Sean Connery

bourgeoisie—but director Michael Gordon is inept. The film keeps aborting its own attempts at scaring the audience by inadvertently making them collapse in giggles. For instance, there is a desperate moment when Lana Turner must drive a car to a rendezvous with Quinn, who is dumping their second murder victim in the ocean. It turns out she can't drive, but is forced to maneuver the car anyway. A scene which might have been harrowing—the ultimate nightmare—turns into a Keystone Kop fest as Turner lurches into traffic and nearly runs down a cable car.

Turner, once again up to her eyeballs in mink, has one lovely costume change after another. No one can believe for a moment that she and Quinn care a fig about one another, despite all their pantings, heavy embraces, and exchanged love talk. But Lana Turner is every inch a star. Pinning a great white orchid on her black sequinned gown, glittering with diamond earrings, bracelet, and matching pin, she flashes her famous dimples and proves to the audience she is the last working movie star who can generate the oldtime glamour.

By Love Possessed (1961) was one of the great literary successes of the fifties, earning its author, James Gould Cozzens, an inflated reputation late in his life. It was inevitable that a film version would be made. Lana Turner was cast as the "beautiful little percolator, all ready to boil over"—the wife of Jason Robards, Jr. The major issue of the plot was how much (or how little) anyone should give in to emotion. Like the blank fifties hungering for the turbulent sixties ahead, the characters keep talking about their dull lives, wishing something—anything—would happen.

Turner makes a spectacular entrance on a spirited horse, to establish her character as a bored housewife who drinks too much but has fire in her blood. She would like to divorce her crippled husband, but he refuses. Love and emotional liberation come to her in the person of Efrem Zimbalist, Jr. . Like most of the women Turner played, this character is bad on the outside but good deep inside—a victim of her beauty and her sex. Wearing a softly curled, cap-like hair style (and more splendid clothes), Turner does what she can to liven up a dull film.

In *By Love Possessed* the elegance of the Ross Hunter productions is missing. The rooms have an empty look, and some of the furniture appears to be from Sears, Roebuck. The screenplay reflects this same emptiness, and lack of class. The film's title, however, was right on target. Following its completion, Lana Turner wed her fifth husband, Fred May, a Los Angeles

IMITATION OF LIFE (1959). With John Gavin

businessman who was said to worship her.

A change of pace awaited Turner in her next two films. Unlike other former stars of the forties, she did not go into horror films. Still youthful and pretty (Turner was only 41 in 1961), a more logical step was into light comedy.

First up was *Bachelor in Paradise* (1961), co-starring Bob Hope. In the sixties Hollywood made a frantic effort to compete with the overt sex in foreign films via double entendre comedies. *Bachelor in Paradise* is the story of a man who writes books on the sex lives of all nations (*How The French Live, How the Swedes Live*, etc.). Because his crooked business manager has left him owing a million in back taxes, Hope takes refuge in a San Fernando Valley housing tract (Paradise Village) to spy on suburban couples and write about how Americans "live." It is a film only a sociologist could love, a short course on the morals and mores of the decade.

The script is funny by fits and starts. Director Jack Arnold is famous for science fiction films, and

IMITATION OF LIFE (1959). As Lora Meredith

he treats the world of southern California exactly as it should be treated—as an alien land. The film is good when ironically depicting a crazy world in which pink is called "California coral," where big brother watches you in the supermarket ("don't squeeze the bread"), and where Muzak is ever-present. Frank Tashlin might have made it into a great film, but Arnold lets it slowly wind down and ultimately fizzle out.

Lana Turner plays a real-estate agent who rents her own home to the writer, played by Hope. (When Hope first learns she is unmarried, he inquires, "Don't they harvest the crops around here?") Hope is un-able to play a person, and his character is nothing but a wise-cracking caricature—a stand-up human being. Turner's character is a superwoman, equally adept at diapering a baby or repairing a tape recorder. She has one delicious moment when, sloshed on Polynesian drinks, she does a slow, sexy hula. For one instant, the Lana Turner of old breaks through the slightly frozen, perfectly coiffed robot *Bachelor in Paradise* makes out of her.

Who's Got the Action? (1962) teams her with Dean Martin in an even more lackluster comedy. This time she's the wife of a successful lawyer (Martin) who likes to play

PORTRAIT IN BLACK (1960). With Anthony Quinn

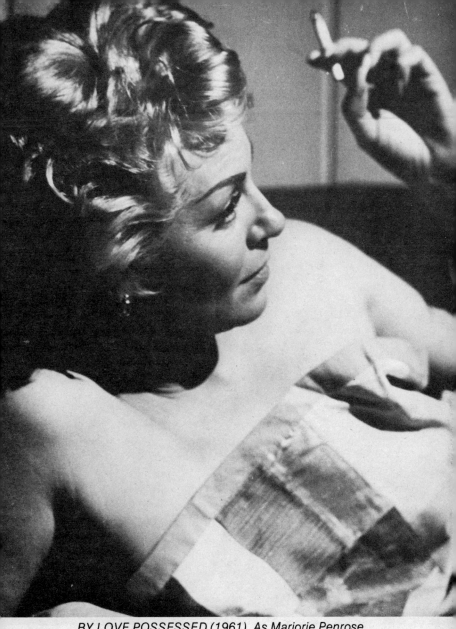
BY LOVE POSSESSED (1961). As Marjorie Penrose

BACHELOR IN PARADISE (1961). With Bob Hope

WHO'S GOT THE ACTION? (1962). With Eddie Albert and Dean Martin

the horses. When she sets out to reform him, she becomes involved with a set of comic bookies masterminded by Walter Matthau in a parody of a tough gangster role.

Dean Martin plays his role at the who-gives-a-damn level. Matthau plays his with the broadest kind of comic satire. Turner tries to play like a professional star determined to do her best no matter what assignment she is given. The result is not only boring, but sad.

Once again, Turner is wending her way through a world of plush apartments, ritzy restaurants, and a maze of costume changes. Looking trim and beautiful, she does what she can with tired material. "You're a kook," people keep saying to her character, but there is no kookiness in her performance—or in her. *Slightly Dangerous* (way back in 1943) had proved she might have been a light comedienne, but that time was long passed. The quality was never developed, or perhaps her tragic personal life made it impossible to accept her as funny. She seems tense and wooden. Her girlish laugh occasionally bursts out, but at this point in her career,

LOVE HAS MANY FACES (1965). With Hugh O'Brian

Turner needs a first-rate director (like Sirk or Minnelli) to show her the way.

Lack of the right man was still a problem in her private life, too. After *Who's Got The Action?*, it was apparent her marriage to May was falling apart. In October, 1962, she obtained a quickie divorce in Juarez, Mexico.

Turner did not make another film until 1964, spending the intervening years reading the many scripts she was submitted (none of which she found appropriate) and filling her professional time with television, considering permanent retirement, and touring with Bob Hope on an 18,000-mile trek through the Far East with his show

for military troops.

Her next film, *Love Has Many Faces* (released in 1965) put her back on familiar ground. Some might even say too familiar. Sunbaked and sleek, Turner plays a rich lady with a shady past. Married to a former beach bum (Cliff Robertson), she tries to keep their love from being destroyed by the bored life they lead in Acapulco. The character is another of those "I spoil everything I touch" women, but she loves Robertson and he loves her. Their relationship is threatened by Hugh O'Brian as a conniving beach boy who wants Turner (and her millions) for himself. He makes a shady living as a gigolo who blackmails his clients

. . . and waits his turn with Lana.

Love Has Many Faces is no worse than some other Turner films. But there is a sadness to it, and to her being in it, that can't go unnoticed. The character she plays panders to what some people believed to be Turner's real self—rich, bored, destructive, and preoccupied with sex. O'Brian's character (his wardrobe is rivalled only by her own) is an obvious Johnny Stompanato type. Turner and Stompanato were known to have vacationed in Acapulco together. He even comments, "She was meant to have seven husbands, and I'm next in line." Scenes of Turner stretched out on a king-sized bed like a human sacrifice in the afternoon light have an eerie quality. The finale, in which she is gored by a bull in her abdomen, is too symbolic to even think about.

Once again, the credits list the men who did the jewels, clothes, and home furnishings. Once again, Turner is dressed to the teeth. Whether wearing a simple black bathing suit topped off with a vivid yellow turban or decked out in a glittery set of blue cocktail shorts

LOVE HAS MANY FACES (1965). As Kit Jordan

with matching stole and jewelry, Turner looks sensational. Critics could say her films were awful—and they did say it—but they had to admit Lana Turner was still somethin' else!

All of Turner's films during this period were panned by critics. However, they rose to new heights insulting the next one, the infamous remake of the old turkey, *Madame X* (1966). This film earned Turner one of the most famous put-downs any actress ever received when critic Pauline Kael wrote, "She's not Madame X, she's Brand X. She's not an actress, she's a commodity." Ironically, Turner plays with absolute conviction, giving a good performance even though the film *is* terrible.

The plot was old-fashioned, even the first time it was filmed. Turner is a wife neglected by her politically important husband (John Forsythe). She is dutiful until one night he is away and she consents to go out with a playboy friend (Ricardo Montalban). They become involved, but she knows "it can't go on this way." On a rainy night, she dons a black fur cape and a good string of pearls and goes to his apartment to tell him so. Unfortunately, he falls down the stairs and dies. Blackmailed by her mother-in-law (Constance Bennett), she is forced to disappear as a mysterious drowning victim, giving up her husband and child. It is the traditional Victorian sacrifice of home and family demanded of the fallen woman. Her life is ruined, and she hits the skids.

MADAME X (1966). With Ricardo Montalban

MADAME X (1966). As Holly Parker

In the big final scene, Turner—down and out and accused of murder—is defended by the grown son who thinks she's dead. Once again put on the witness stand, Turner gives a touching performance that in earlier times would have earned her an Oscar. (Several actresses *did* win Oscars for sillier films and lesser performances.) Turner celebrated the film's completion in what was becoming almost a traditional way: she got married. This time it was another young man about town who neglected to mention a previous marriage (although he *was* legally divorced): Robert Eaton, number six.

Although her name was as big as ever, the difficulty of finding suitable roles—the problem of all female stars—finally caught up with Turner. She was off the screen for a period of three years, coming back to make a disastrous film shot in Mexico and titled *The Big Cube* (1969).

"This is a pop art world, baby," advises one young swinger to a

THE BIG CUBE (1969). With Dan O'Herlihy

friend in an early scene of *The Big Cube*. No better explanation of one of the worst films ever made could be given. After thirty-two years in the business, Lana Turner looks less than gorgeous on film for the first time. Playing the role of a famous actress, Turner wears an expensive wardrobe, but is undermined by a series of gorgonlike wigs, knee high boots that belong on a teen-ager, and armloads of jewelry.

Suddenly it is as if Lana Turner herself has undergone the *Imitation of Life* credits sequence. At first one jewel—then two or three—and finally a basketful—is dropped on her until she ends up looking false and unreal, an imitation of Lana Turner. Or, worse, an imitation of Mae West.

In *The Big Cube*, Turner's stepdaughter falls under the spell of an unscrupulous young man (George Chakiris) who produces LSD in the chemistry lab at college. The two try to induce Turner to kill herself by lacing her medicine with acid so that she has a series of psychedelic nightmares.

It is almost impossible to do jus-

PERSECUTION (1973). With Mark Weavers

With fifth husband Fred May

tice to how bad *The Big Cube* really is. It is a prime example of sixties culture as interpreted by the middle-aged. Its final scene has George Chakiris crawling around a slum dwelling, searching for the sugar cubes he has laced with LSD and spilled in his haste to consume them. (An entire bowlful of sugar cubes!) When he comes across a tiny ant trying to move one of the cubes, he picks it up between his fingertips and philosophizes, "No, no, little ant. It's bad for you." The same might be said for the film.

The Big Cube would seem to be as bad as a film could be, but Turner, as always, could surprise her audiences. Her last film to date, *Persecution* (1973), also released as *Sheba*, and *The Terror of Sheba*, was by her own admission even worse. ("A disaster," she called it.) She plays a nasty woman who does in her husband and then tries to destroy the life of her son, only to be murdered by the vengeful lad. The film was so bad that she insisted it not be released. Film historian William K. Everson, one of the few to see it, reports that in this movie, Turner is hypnotized and made to pretend she's a cat, getting down on all fours to lap up a saucer of milk. What a way for the kittenish little girl from the soda fountain stool to end up.

The poor films weren't all of it, either. Alas, Lana Turner's penchant for unfortunate marriages had continued. After the Stompanato trial, she did manage to bounce back and revitalize her career, even if some of the movies were not listed among the ten best of the year. Her personal life, however, could only be described, even by those who love her, as a mess. It was a decade of confusion for Lana Turner, particularly during Cheryl's difficult years of adjustment. She had wed and divorced both Fred May and Robert Eaton, but had outdone herself with number seven, a nightclub hypnotist she had only known three weeks. He, too, forgot to mention a former marriage, as well as to give his right name (Ronald Peller).

Perhaps the *New York Times* Index can tell it best:

TURNER, L.: To wed F. May 8/31/60
Weds. F. May 11/28/60
Divorces F. May 10/17/62
Fires at but misses prowler in Malibu home 7/21/64
Weds R.P. Eaton 6/8/65
Ill 7/7/65
Seeks divorce from R.P. Eaton, her sixth husband 7/15/67
Divorces R.P. Eaton 4/2/69
Weds night club hypnotist R. Dante 5/9/69

With sixth husband Robert Eaton

Dante shot at by gunmen in Hollywood 7/18/69
SEE
MURDERS—ARIZONA

Under this final entry was recorded the sordid details of Lana Turner's seventh husband's attempt to kill a fellow hypnotist somewhere in Arizona. Dante's trial was postponed so that he could undergo mental tests. The examining psychiatrist had contended that Dante's mental faculties might have been damaged by drugs. After a marriage of six months—her shortest since Artie Shaw—Lana Turner separated from Number Seven.

With Ronald Dante, Lana Turner had reached the bottom of a long descent into the marriage bin. In late 1969, she brought suit against him, accusing him of defrauding her of $34,000. In addition she received the gloomy news that a television series she was appearing in, *The Survivors*, would not itself survive. This show, launched on September 29, 1969, had been one of Lana's hopes for a new lease on her career. She did not need money—besides the income from her films, she owned land and several winning race horses—but she did need something to do professionally. ("I need activity," said Turner. "Oh God, how I need activity.") With a seventh marriage collapsed in ashes, a

BITTERSWEET LOVE (1976). With Robert Lansing

television series down the drain, and no film in sight, everything was coming up dandelions.

Just as things looked hopeless, early in 1971, Lana was approached about the possibility of appearing in summer stock. She was invited to star in the popular Broadway comedy, *Forty Carats*, the story of a forty-year-old woman who falls in love with a much younger man. Always a shrewd businesswoman, Turner forged a deal that brought her nearly $200,-000 . . . plus the guarantee of salaries for her personal hairdresser, make-up man, chauffeur and limousine. All over Hollywood, scoffers scoffed and laughers laughed, predicting she'd never make it. She'd be too frightened. She'd forget her lines. No one would pay to see her. Turner was a movie queen, they said, but not a stage actress.

True to her tradition, however, Lana Turner did make it. She was a huge success, and it looked like the beginning of a whole new career. Not only did requests to do more legitimate theater come her way, but her stage success brought in new offers for television and films, as well.

The final index entry to date under Turner's name reads as follows:

TURNER, L.: Tribute to will be presented at Town Hall Lana Turner in person to hostess 4/13/75

It was a sell-out, including standing room. She walked in to a prolonged standing ovation, every inch the glamour girl, star of screen, radio, television and stage. Lana Turner was still Lana Turner.

Sometime in the thirties an old beat-up Star automobile (the only car on the market cheaper than a Model-T) drifted down a California highway, headed toward San Francisco. In the back seat, sound asleep, was a dark-haired young woman. Up front at the wheel, but also sleeping, sat a handsome man. In his lap, steering for all she was worth was a little girl with a pink hair ribbon—Miss Judy Turner.

According to various sources, Lana Turner has described this incident as one of her earliest childhood memories. "I believe that such incidents in early childhood have a great bearing on what you are like and how you behave in later life. I was applauded for taking over in an emergency. I learned that was the thing to do."

The question is: did it ever really happen? It seems possible that the event might be a recurring nightmare of a little girl whose father was murdered and whose mother was forced to board her out with strangers. Or even of a teen-age kid who had to support her family by way of sex appeal and good looks. While she was still too young to be in charge, before anyone had taught her what she needed to know, Lana Turner found herself up front in the spotlight, driving the car as best as she could: "Almost from that day my life has been a series of emergencies in which I have had to take

THE SURVIVOR

the wheel without knowing where I was going or how to run the machine."

Some who lead difficult lives endure. Endurance implies a triumph over destructive forces as well as an innocence on the part of the victim. Others merely survive, managing to hang on in a whirlwind that is possibly of their own creation. They are buffeted about, but never beaten. They can take it. Lana Turner is one of those survivors.

No one is going to say she has lived a sensible life. But what *can* be said is that the personal characteristics that have enabled her to live through her own mistakes are rarely noted. Turner has a wry sense of humor that she can train on herself as well as anyone else. She can even make jokes about her husbands. When she first heard an ex was going to marry a skater, she dimpled and said, "Well, she must have taught him how to skate. He never skated with me." When asked why she had ever married Ronald Dante, she commented, "If they're clever and they give me the right story, I take the bait." On her relations with newsmen, Turner laughs, "The Hollywood press has been good to me. They've always crucified me with a smile."

Besides humor, Turner has

everything she was criticized for without a flash of temper. When she was accused of over-indulging her only daughter with a fur coat when the girl was only three-and-a-half, Lana snapped, "No! She was two-and-a-half, and the coat had a matching ermine halo hat and she had handmade French white glacé gloves because when this child was out of her pajamas, she was *dressed*!"

She understood and accepted the realities of her goldfish bowl life: "When a small town girl makes a mistake, her family covers up for her. But me, nobody covers up for me." She realized that this was a price she had to pay for stardom: "We are unconscious of what Hollywood may do to us. At the same time, it is unfair to blame this on Hollywood ... I know, of course, that my love affair with Crane, my quick remarriage because of my child, and then a divorce—I know these matters must have seemed hilariously funny, the irresponsible antics of Hollywood people of no character. I can blame no one."

She was always known to be vulnerable: "Why do people want to hurt me? I can't understand it." She kept that softness, because she was a kind person basically, but she finally worked out her own private rules to live by: "Never look back is my philosophy. What's past is past, and I can't let it destroy me ... I must continue working. The fact is that it's the only thing I know."

She never *did* look back. She had youth on her side (she was discovered when she was only fifteen, after all), as well as a basic resilience and a durable constitution. Although she may have led a disastrous private life, she kept going, kept trying to make it better. Lana Turner was always looking ahead, watching for that "something good is just around the corner" that usually turned out to be a pie in the face ... or worse. She was never found whining to the press about how tough things were when she was young. She didn't kill herself. She didn't end up waiting tables in a small town beanery. She wasn't found down-and-out in Bellevue. Unlike the High Priestess in *The Prodigal*, she refused to leap into the flames.

On the contrary, residents of Los Angeles recently noticed a film crew, on location in downtown city streets. Shooting was underway, and the camera was making a long track beside an elegant and beautiful woman. Her head-up, hip-swinging walk seemed familiar ... it was Lana Turner, making *Bittersweet Love*, her latest feature movie, still before the cameras, still working, and still looking good.

Who knows? Maybe she will live to be 100. Long after the last glamour girl has fallen arches—or yel-

lowed scrapbooks—or a name too forgotten even for the "where they are now" vultures, maybe Lana Turner will still be working. Perhaps someday she'll be honored as the Grand Champion Glamour Girl of them all.

No doubt she'll come in person to accept the award. She'll walk down a set of Ziegfeld stairs, tramp across a stage laid with mink skins, and step right up into the spotlight. She'll be loaded with diamonds and looking fifty years younger than she is, hair all platinum and a dazzling smile on her face. She won't have to do or say a thing . . . just stand there and wait for the whistles. It'll be little Julia Jean Mildred Frances Turner Shaw Crane Topping Barker May Eaton Dante *Whoever*. The Survivor.

Maybe this time something good really *is* around the corner . . .

BIBLIOGRAPHY

Barthel, J., "Survivor on TV: Lana," *Life*, September 26, 1969.

Bell, Arthur, "Interview With Lana Turner," *New York Times* Arts and Leisure Section, June 27, 1971.

Busch, Niven, "Lana Turner," *Life*, December 23, 1940.

Crane, Cheryl Christina (sic), "Speaking Up—I'm Hollywood's Newest Pin-Up Girl," *Photoplay*, December, 1943.

"Death on a Pink Carpet," *Time*, April 14, 1958.

Hamilton, Sara, "Lana's Baby," *Photoplay*, March, 1943.

Howe, Herb, "Lana—and Howe!" *Photoplay*, February, 1947.

Kilgallen, Dorothy, "Lana Does It Again," *Modern Screen*, March, 1948.

"Lana's Plea," *Life*, April 21, 1958.

"Lana Turner Scrap Book," *Photoplay*, October, 1944.

"Lana's Fourth and Positively Last Time," *Life*, May 10, 1948.

LeRoy, Mervyn, as told to Dick Kleiner, *Mervyn LeRoy: Take One*, Hawthorne Books, New York, 1974.

"Marriage Is A Private Affair," (Film Plot), *Modern Screen*, August, 1944.

Miller, Cynthia, "What Now, Lana?" *Modern Screen*, July, 1944.

Morella, Joe and Epstein, Edward Z., *Lana: The Private and Public Lives of Miss Turner*, Citadel Press, New York, 1971.

Parish, James Robert, *Hollywood's Great Love-Teams*, "Gable and Turner," Arlington House, 1974.

Parish, James Robert and Bowers, Ronald, *The MGM Stock Company*, "Lana Turner," Arlington House, 1973.

Parsons, Louella O., "And So Goodbye," *Photoplay*, February, 1946.

———. "Diamonds and Diapers," *Photoplay*, February, 1949.

———. "The Fabulous Mrs. Topping," *Photoplay*, November, 1950.

———. "I've Waited All My Life," *Photoplay*, July, 1948.

———. "Lana Talks About Turhan," *Photoplay*, April, 1945.

———. *Tell It To Louella*, Lancer Books, New York, 1961.

Pieck, Kaaren, "Golden Girl," *Modern Screen*, November, 1947.

St. Johns, Adela Rogers, "Lana!" *Photoplay*, September, 1945.

Smith, Robert, *Douglas Sirk: The Complete American Period*, "Notes on Imitation of Life," University of Connecticut Publications, 1974.

Squire, Nancy Winslow, "The Strange Case of Lana Turner," *Modern Screen*, May, 1943.

"Sweater Girl's Build Up To Tragedy," *Life*, April 14, 1958.

Thompson, Howard, "Lana Turner Is The Only Security," *New York Times* Arts and Leisure Section, March 13, 1966.

"Tragic Life of a Star," *Newsweek*, April 14, 1958.

Turner, Lana, "My Private Life," *Woman's Home Companion*, December, 1951.

Valentino, Lou, *The Films of Lana Turner*, Citadel Press, 1976.

Wallace, Irving, "The Loves of Lana Turner," *Liberty*, September 5, 1942.

West, Rosemary, "Lana's Madcap Marriage," *Photoplay*, October, 1942.

Zeitlin, Ida, "Lana Turner's Life Story, Parts I and II," *Modern Screen*, February and March, 1944.

THE FILMS OF LANA TURNER

The director's name follows the release date. A (c) following the release date in-dicates the film was in color. Sp indicates screenplay and b/o indicates based/on.

1. A STAR IS BORN. Selznick-International, United Artists, 1937 (c). *William A. Wellman.* Sp: Dorothy Parker, Alan Campbell, and Robert Carson, b/o story by William A. Wellman and Robert Carson. Cast: Fredric March, Janet Gaynor, Adolphe Menjou, May Robson, Andy Devine, Lionel Stander, Elizabeth Jenns, Edgar Kennedy, Owen Moore, Arthur Hoyt, Guinn (Big Boy) Williams, Vince Barnett, Franklin Pangborn. Remade in 1954 and 1976.

2. THEY WON'T FORGET. Warner Brothers/First National, 1937. *Mervyn LeRoy.* Sp: Robert Rossen and Aben Kandel, b/o novel "Death in the Deep South," by Ward Greene. Cast: Claude Rains, Gloria Dickson, Edward Norris, Otto Kruger, Allyn Joslyn, Elisha Cook, Jr., Cy Kendall, Elisabeth Risdon, Eddie Acuff.

3. THE GREAT GARRICK. Warner Brothers/First National, 1937. *James Whale.* Sp: Ernest Vajda, b/o his story "Ladies and Gentlemen." Cast: Brian Aherne, Olivia de Havilland, Edward Everett Horton, Melville Cooper, Henry O'Neill, Lionel Atwill, Luis Alberni, Marie Wilson, Etienne Girardot, Dorothy Tree, Fritz Lieber.

4. THE ADVENTURES OF MARCO POLO. A Samuel Goldwyn Production, released by United Artists, 1938. *Archie Mayo.* Sp: Robert E. Sherwood, b/o story by N. A. Pogson. Cast: Gary Cooper, Sigrid Gurie, Basil Rathbone, Ernest Truex, Alan Hale, George Barbier, Binnie Barnes, Stanley Fields, H.B. Warner, Henry Kolker.

5. LOVE FINDS ANDY HARDY. MGM, 1938. *George B. Seitz.* Sp: William Ludwig, b/o stories by Vivien R. Bretherton and characters by Aurania Rouverol. Cast: Mickey Rooney, Lewis Stone, Judy Garland, Ann Rutherford, Cecilia Parker, Fay Holden.

6. THE CHASER. MGM, 1938. *Edwin L. Marin.* Sp: Everett Freeman, Harry Ruskin, and Sam and Bella Spewack, b/o story by Chandler Sprague and Howard Emmett Rogers. Cast: Dennis O'Keefe, Ann Morriss, Lewis Stone, Nat Pendleton, Henry O'Neill, John Qualen. A remake of *The Nuisance* (1933).

7. RICH MAN, POOR GIRL. MGM, 1938. *Reinhold Schunzel.* Sp: Joseph A. Fields and Jerome Chodorov, b/o story by Edgar Franklin. Cast: Robert Young, Lew Ayres, Ruth Hussey, Rita Johnson, Don Castle, Guy Kibbee, Virginia Grey, Marie Blake.

8.   DRAMATIC SCHOOL. MGM, 1938. *Robert B. Sinclair*. Sp: Ernest Vajda and Mary McCall, Jr., b/o Hungarian play, "School for Drama" by Hans Szekely and Zoltan Egyed. Cast: Luise Rainer, Paulette Goddard, Ann Rutherford, Gale Sondergaard, Margaret Dumont, Alan Marshal, Henry Stephenson, Melville Cooper, Genevieve Tobin, Erik Rhodes, Marie Blake, Rand Brooks, Virginia Grey.

9.   CALLING DR. KILDARE. MGM, 1939. *Harold S. Bucquet*. Sp: Harry Ruskin and David Goldbeck, b/o story by Max Brand. Cast: Lew Ayres, Lionel Barrymore, Laraine Day, Nat Pendleton, Samuel S. Hinds, Emma Dunn, Alma Kruger, Marie Blake, Phillip Terry, Donald Barry.

10.   THESE GLAMOUR GIRLS. MGM, 1939. *S. Sylvan Simon*. Sp: Jane Hall and Marion Parsonnet, b/o Cosmopolitan magazine story by Jane Hall. Cast: Jane Bryan, Anita Louise, Ann Rutherford, Lew Ayres, Marsha Hunt, Mary Beth Hughes, Tom Brown, Ernest Truex, Richard Carlson.

11.   DANCING CO-ED. MGM, 1939. *S. Sylvan Simon*. Sp: Albert Mannheimer, b/o story by Albert Treynor. Cast: Richard Carlson, Artie Shaw, Ann Rutherford, Lee Bowman, Thurston Hall, Leon Errol, Roscoe Karns, Mary Beth Hughes, June Preisser, Monty Woolley.

12.   TWO GIRLS ON BROADWAY. MGM, 1940. *S. Sylvan Simon*. Sp: Joseph Fields and Jerome Chodorov, b/o story by Edmund Goulding. Cast: Joan Blondell, George Murphy, Kent Taylor, Wallace Ford, Lloyd Corrigan, Don Wilson. A remake of *The Broadway Melody* (1929).

13.   WE WHO ARE YOUNG. MGM, 1940. *Harold S. Bucquet*. Sp: Dalton Trumbo, b/o his own story. Cast: John Shelton, Gene Lockhart, Grant Mitchell, Ian Wolfe, Henry Armetta, Jonathan Hale.

14.   ZIEGFELD GIRL. MGM, 1941. *Robert Z. Leonard*. Sp: Marguerite Roberts and Sonya Levien, b/o original story by William Anthony McGuire. Cast: James Stewart, Judy Garland, Hedy Lamarr, Tony Martin, Dan Dailey, Charles Winninger, Philip Dorn, Jackie Cooper, Eve Arden, Ian Hunter, Edward Everett Horton, Paul Kelly, Al Shean, Felix Bressart.

15.   DR. JEKYLL AND MR. HYDE. MGM, 1941. *Victor Fleming*. Sp: John Lee Mahin, b/o the novel by Robert Louis Stevenson. Cast: Spencer Tracy, Ingrid Bergman, Donald Crisp, Barton MacLane, C. Aubrey Smith, Sara Allgood, Ian Hunter, Peter Godfrey, Billy Bevan. Previously filmed in 1920 and 1932.

16.   HONKY TONK. MGM, 1941. *Jack Conway*. Sp: Marguerite Roberts and John Sanford. Cast: Clark Gable, Claire Trevor, Frank Morgan, Marjorie Main, Albert Dekker, Chill Wills, Henry O'Neill, Veda Ann Borg, Douglas Wood.

17.   JOHNNY EAGER. MGM, 1941. *Mervyn LeRoy*. Sp: John Lee Mahin and Edward Grant, b/o original story by Grant. Cast: Robert Taylor, Edward Arnold, Van Heflin, Robert Sterling, Patricia Dane, Glenda Farrell, Henry O'Neill, Diana Lewis, Barry Nelson, Charles Dingle, Paul Stewart, Connie Gilchrist.

18.   SOMEWHERE I'LL FIND YOU. MGM, 1942. *Wesley Ruggles*. Sp: Marguerite Roberts, b/o Walter Reisch's adaptation of story by Charles Hoffman. Cast: Clark Gable, Robert Sterling, Patricia Dane, Reginald Owen, Lee Patrick, Charles Dingle.

19.   THE YOUNGEST PROFESSION. MGM, 1943. *Edward Buzzell*. Sp: George Oppenheimer, Charles Lederer, and Leonard Spigelgass, b/o book by Lillian Day. Cast: Virginia Weidler, Edward Arnold, John Carroll, with guest appearances by Greer Garson, Walter Pidgeon, Robert Taylor, William Powell.

20.   SLIGHTLY DANGEROUS. MGM, 1943. *Wesley Ruggles*. Sp: Charles Lederer and George Oppenheimer, b/o story by Ian McLellan Hunter and Aileen Hamilton. Cast: Robert Young, Walter Brennan, Dame May Whitty, Eugene Pallette, Florence Bates, Alan Mowbray, Bobby Blake.

21.   DU BARRY WAS A LADY. MGM, 1943 (c). *Roy Del Ruth*. Sp: Irving Brecher, adapted by Nancy Hamilton and b/o musical play by Herbert Fields and B.G. DeSylva. Cast: Red Skelton, Gene Kelly, Lucille Ball, Virginia O'Brien, Rags Ragland, Zero Mostel, Donald Meek, Douglass Dumbrille, Louise Beavers, and Tommy Dorsey and his Orchestra. Guest appearance.

22.   MARRIAGE IS A PRIVATE AFFAIR. MGM, 1944. *Robert Z. Leonard*. Sp: David Hertz and Lenore Coffee, b/o novel by Judith Kelly. Cast: James Craig, John Hodiak, Frances Gifford, Hugh Marlowe, Natalie Schafer, Keenan Wynn, Herbert Rudley, Paul Cavanagh, Morris Ankrum, Jane Greer, Tom Drake.

23.   KEEP YOUR POWDER DRY. MGM, 1945. *Edward Buzzell*. Sp: Mary McCall, Jr. and George Bruce. Cast: Laraine Day, Susan Peters, Agnes Moorehead, Bill Johnson, Natalie Schafer, Lee Patrick, Jess Barker, June Lockhart.

24.   WEEKEND AT THE WALDORF. MGM. 1945. *Robert Z. Leonard*. Sp: Sam and Bella Spewark, b/o adaptation by Guy Bolton, and suggested by play by Vicki Baum. Cast: Ginger Rogers, Walter Pidgeon, Van Johnson, Keenan Wynn, Edward Arnold, Robert Benchley, Phyllis Thaxter, Xavier Cugat and his Orchestra, Lina Romay, Samuel S. Hinds. A remake of *Grand Hotel* (1932).

25.   THE POSTMAN ALWAYS RINGS TWICE. MGM, 1946. *Tay Garnett*. Sp: Harry Ruskin and Niven Busch, b/o novel by James M. Cain. Cast: John Garfield, Cecil Kellaway, Hume Cronyn, Leon Ames, Audrey Totter, Alan Reed, Jeff York.

26. GREEN DOLPHIN STREET. MGM, 1947. *Victor Saville.* Sp: Samson Raphaelson, b/o prize-winning novel by Elizabeth Goudge. Cast: Donna Reed, Richard Hart, Van Heflin, Frank Morgan, Edmund Gwenn, Gladys Cooper, Dame May Whitty, Reginald Owen, Moyna Macgill, Linda Christian, Gigi Perreau.

27. CASS TIMBERLANE. MGM, 1947. *George Sidney.* Sp: Donald Ogden Stewart, from adaptation by Stewart and Sonya Levien, b/o novel by Sinclair Lewis. Cast: Spencer Tracy, Mary Astor, Zachary Scott, Tom Drake, Albert Dekker, Cameron Mitchell, Margaret Lindsay, John Litel, Mona Barrie, Selena Royle, Josephine Hutchinson.

28. HOMECOMING. MGM, 1948. *Mervyn LeRoy.* Sp: Paul Osborn, from adaptation by Jan Lustig, b/o original story by Sidney Kingsley. Cast: Clark Gable, Anne Baxter, John Hodiak, Ray Collins, Cameron Mitchell, Gladys Cooper, Marshall Thompson.

29. THE THREE MUSKETEERS. MGM, 1948 (c). *George Sidney.* Sp: Robert Ardrey, b/o novel by Alexandre Dumas. Cast: Gene Kelly, June Allyson, Van Heflin, Angela Lansbury, Frank Morgan, Vincent Price, Keenan Wynn, John Sutton, Gig Young, Robert Coote, Reginald Owen, Ian Keith, Patricia Medina, and Richard Stapley. Other versions in 1914, 1921, 1935, and 1939. Remade in 1974.

30. A LIFE OF HER OWN. MGM, 1950. *George Cukor.* Sp: Isobel Lennart. Cast: Ray Milland, Louis Calhern, Ann Dvorak, Tom Ewell, Barry Sullivan, Margaret Phillips, Jean Hagen.

31. MR. IMPERIUM. MGM, 1951 (c). *Don Hartman.* Sp: Edwin H. Knopf and Don Hartman, b/o play by Edwin H. Knopf. Cast: Ezio Pinza, Marjorie Main, Debbie Reynolds, Barry Sullivan, Cedric Hardwicke, Ann Codee.

32. THE MERRY WIDOW. MGM, 1952 (c). *Curtis Bernhardt.* Sp: Sonya Levien and William Ludwig, b/o operetta by Franz Lehar, Victor Leon, and Leo Stein. Cast: Fernando Lamas, Una Merkel, Richard Haydn, Thomas Gomez, John Abbott, Marcel Dalio, King Donovan, Robert Coote, Ludwig Stossel. Other versions in 1925 and 1934.

33. THE BAD AND THE BEAUTIFUL. MGM, 1952. *Vincente Minnelli.* Sp: Charles Schnee, b/o story by David Bradshaw. Cast: Kirk Douglas, Dick Powell, Gloria Grahame, Walter Pidgeon, Gilbert Roland, Barry Sullivan, Elaine Stewart, Leo G. Carroll, Vanessa Brown, Paul Stewart, Sammy White.

34. LATIN LOVERS. MGM, 1953 (c). *Mervyn LeRoy.* Sp: Isobel Lennart. Cast: John Lund, Ricardo Montalban, Jean Hagen, Louis Calhern, Eduard Franz, Beulah Bondi, Rita Moreno, Joaquin Garay.

35. THE FLAME AND THE FLESH. MGM, 1954 (c). *Richard Brooks*. Sp: Helen Deutsch, b/o novel by Auguste Bailly. Cast: Carlos Thompson, Pier Angeli, Eric Pohlmann, Bonar Colleano, Charles Goldner, Peter Illing.

36. BETRAYED. MGM, 1954 (c). *Gottfried Reinhardt*. Sp: Ronald Millar and George Froeschel. Cast: Clark Gable, Victor Mature, O.E. Hasse, Wilfrid Hyde-White, Ian Carmichael, Niall MacGinnis, Nora Swinburne, Roland Culver.

37. THE PRODIGAL. MGM, 1955 (c). *Richard Thorpe*. Sp: Maurice Zimm, b/o adaptation of the Bible stories by Joe Breen, Jr. and Samuel James Larsen. Cast: Edmund Purdom, James Mitchell, Louis Calhern, Taina Elg, Francis L. Sullivan, Audrey Dalton, Neville Brand, Walter Hampden, Joseph Wiseman, John Dehner, Cecil Kellaway.

38. THE SEA CHASE. Warner Brothers, 1955 (c). *John Farrow*. Sp: James Warner Bellah and John Twist, b/o novel by Andrew Geer. Cast: John Wayne, Lyle Bettger, David Farrar, Tab Hunter, James Arness, Richard Davalos, John Qualen, Paul Fix, Alan Hale.

39. THE RAINS OF RANCHIPUR. Twentieth Century Fox, 1955 (c). *Jean Negulesco*. Sp: Merle Miller, b/o novel by Louis Bromfield. Cast: Richard Burton, Michael Rennie, Fred MacMurray, Joan Caulfield, Eugenie Leontovitch, Madge Kennedy, Gladys Hurlburt. A remake of *The Rains Came* (1939).

40. DIANE. MGM, 1955 (c). *David Miller*. Sp: Christopher Isherwood, b/o story "Diane de Poitiers" by John Erskine. Cast: Marisa Pavan, Cedric Hardwicke, Roger Moore, Pedro Armendariz, Torin Thatcher, Taina Elg, Henry Daniell, Melville Cooper, John Lupton.

41. PEYTON PLACE. Twentieth Century Fox, 1957 (c). *Mark Robson*. Sp: John Michael Hayes, b/o novel by Grace Metalious. Cast: Hope Lange, Arthur Kennedy, Betty Field, Lloyd Nolan, Diane Varsi, Terry Moore, Leon Ames, Lee Philips, Russ Tamblyn, Barry Coe, David Nelson, Mildred Dunnock, Lorne Greene.

42. THE LADY TAKES A FLYER. Universal, 1958 (c). *Jack Arnold*. Sp: Danny Arnold, b/o story by Edmund H. North. Cast: Jeff Chandler, Chuck Connors, Richard Denning, Nestor Paiva, Andra Martin, Reta Shaw, Jerry Paris.

43. ANOTHER TIME, ANOTHER PLACE. Paramount, 1958. A Kaydor Production. *Lewis Allen*. Sp: Stanley Mann, b/o novel by Lenore Coffee. Cast: Sean Connery, Barry Sullivan, Glynis Johns, Terence Longden, Sidney James, Doris Hare, Martin Stephens.

44. IMITATION OF LIFE. Universal, 1959 (c). *Douglas Sirk*. Sp: Eleanore Griffin and Allan Scott, b/o novel by Fannie Hurst. Cast: John Gavin, Sandra Dee, Juanita Moore, Susan Kohner, Dan O'Herlihy, Robert Alda, Troy Donahue, Mahalia Jackson. Previously filmed in 1934.

45. PORTRAIT IN BLACK. Universal, 1960 (c). *Michael Gordon*. Sp: Ivan Goff and Ben Roberts, b/o play by Goff and Roberts. Cast: Anthony Quinn, Sandra Dee, John Saxon, Lloyd Nolan, Richard Basehart, Anna May Wong, Ray Walston.

46. BY LOVE POSSESSED. United Artists, 1961 (c). *John Sturges*. Sp. Charles Schnee, b/o novel by James Gould Cozzens. Cast: Efrem Zimbalist Jr., Susan Kohner, Jason Robards, Jr., Thomas Mitchell, George Hamilton, Barbara Bel Geddes, Yvonne Craig, Everett Sloane, Reta Shaw, John McGiver, Janis Paige, Jim Hutton.

47. BACHELOR IN PARADISE. MGM, 1961 (c). *Jack Arnold*. Sp: Valentine Davies and Hal Kanter, b/o story by Vera Caspary. Cast: Bob Hope, Paula Prentiss, Virginia Grey, Don Porter, Agnes Moorehead, Clinton Sundberg.

48. WHO'S GOT THE ACTION? Paramount, 1962 (c). *Daniel Mann*. Sp: Jack Rose, b/o novel *"Four Horse Players are Missing,"* by Alexander Rose. Cast: Dean Martin, Walter Matthau, Nita Talbot, Margo, Eddie Albert, Paul Ford, John McGiver.

49. LOVE HAS MANY FACES. Columbia, 1965 (c). *Alexander Singer*. Sp: Marguerite Roberts. Cast: Cliff Robertson, Hugh O'Brian, Ruth Roman, Virginia Grey, Carlos Montalban, Stephanie Powers, Ron Husmann.

50. MADAME X. Universal, 1966 (c). *David Lowell Rich*. Sp: Jean Holloway, b/o play by Alexandre Brisson. Cast: John Forsythe, Constance Bennett, Keir Dullea, Ricardo Montalban, Burgess Meredith, John Van Dreelan, Virginia Grey. Previously filmed in 1920, 1929, and 1937.

51. THE BIG CUBE. Warner Brothers-7 Arts, 1969 (c). *Tito Davison*. Sp: William Douglas Lansford, b/o story by Tito Davison and Edmundo Baez. Cast: Dan O'Herlihy, George Chakiris, Richard Egan, Karin Mossberg, Pamela Rodgers.

52. PERSECUTION (also released as SHEBA and THE TERROR OF SHEBA), Tyburn Films, 1973 (c). *Don Chaffey*. Sp: Robert B. Hutton, b/o his story. Cast: Ralph Bates, Trevor Howard, Olga Georges-Picot, Susan Farmer.

53. BITTERSWEET LOVE. A Zappala-Slott Production, 1976 (c). *David Miller*. Sp: Adrian Morrall and D. A. Kellogg. Cast: Celeste Holm, Robert Alda, Robert Lansing, Scott Hylands, Meredith Baxter Birney.

INDEX

156

ABOUT THE AUTHOR

Jeanine Basinger is an Associate Professor of Film at Wesleyan University in Middletown, Connecticut, where she teaches courses on all aspects of American film history and aesthetics. She is the author of two other volumes in the Pyramid Illustrated History of the Movies: *Shirley Temple* and *Gene Kelly*. In addition, her articles have appeared in numerous publications, including the *New York Times, American Film*, and in several anthologies, including *The Movie Buff's Book* and *The Movie Buff's Book: Two*.

ABOUT THE EDITOR

Ted Sennett is the author of *Warner Brothers Presents*, a tribute to the great Warners films of the thirties and forties, and of *Lunatics and Lovers*, on the long-vanished but well-remembered "screwball" movie comedies of the past. He is also the editor of *The Movie Buff's Book, The Old-Time Radio Book*, and *The Movie Buff's Book: Two*.

Pyramid's Illustrated History of the Movies

a beautiful, original series of enchanting volumes on your favorite stars and motion pictures. Each book is superbly written and contains dozens of exciting photos! They are available from your local dealer, or you can use this page to order direct.

groom was scathingly referred to by *Life* magazine as "considered very talented by cafe society . . . because he inherited $7 million and plays a fine game of golf."

The wedding itself was thoroughly ridiculed by *Life* in a story entitled "For the Fourth and Definitely Last Time."* Turner's lifelong friend, Billy Wilkerson, acted as host for the reception and also as Topping's best man. Completely ignoring his close connection with Turner, *Life* pointed out that Wilkerson "moved in upper circles by virtue of having risen from speakeasy manager to publisher of the *Hollywood Reporter*—an expert on marriages, having engaged in five of them himself."

Despite newspaper cruelty and cynicism, the bride was starry-eyed and beautiful. Wearing champagne lace, fortified by a $30,000

*Although Topping was Turner's third husband, it was her fourth marriage.

With third husband Bob Topping

With Cheryl in 1945